Running for Women

RUNNING
FOR WOMEN

DITCH THE EXCUSES AND START LOVING YOUR RUN

DANICA NEWON

ROCKRIDGE
PRESS

To Bryan and Cora
May our life together be an incredible journey to the finish line.

For general information on our other products and services or to obtain technical support, please contact our Customer Care Department within the U.S. at (866) 744-2665, or outside the U.S. at (510) 253-0500.

Rockridge Press publishes its books in a variety of electronic and print formats. Some content that appears in print may not be available in electronic books, and vice versa.

TRADEMARKS: Rockridge Press and the Rockridge Press logo are trademarks or registered trademarks of Callisto Media Inc. and/or its affiliates, in the United States and other countries, and may not be used without written permission. All other trademarks are the property of their respective owners. Rockridge Press is not associated with any product or vendor mentioned in this book.

Photography © Izf/iStock, p.2–3; Lumina/Stocksy, p.5; BONNINSTUDIO/Stocksy, p.6; Izf/iStock, p.8–9; Lumina/Stocksy, p.11; pixdeluxe/iStock, p.15; andresr/iStock, p.16–17; nullplus/iStock, p.19; Studio Firma/Stocksy, p.21; Renee Moora Ferri, p.23; piranka/iStock, p.25; Cara Slifka/Stocksy, p.27; Shaun Robinson/Stocksy, p.28–29; Maridav/Shutterstock, p.31; BONNINSTUDIO/Stocksy, p.33; BraunS/iStock, p.35; Jacob Lund/Stocksy, p.37; Leadinglights/iStock, p.38; Petar Chernaev/iStock, p.41; Nils Nilsen, p. 43; Studio Firma/Stocksy, p.44–45; kurga/iStock, p.46; Gabriel (Gabi) Bucataru/Stocksy, p.56–57; Harald Walker/Stocksy, p.61; Antonio_Diaz/iStock, p.62; Philip Webb/StockFood, p.65; Ian Garlick/StockFood, p. 68; Lindsay Alexander, p. 71; Lee Avison/Stocksy, p.72; Orsolya Bán/Stocksy, p.79; Jacob Lund/Stocksy, p.80–81; petesaloutos/iStock, p.89; Christopher Futcher/iStock, p.90–91; padu_foto/Shutterstock, p.92; Nils Nilsen, p. 95; padu_foto/Shutterstock, p.97; Halfpoint/Shutterstock, p.99; Petar Chernaev/iStock, front cover and p.100

Illustrations © 2015 by Tom Bingham

ISBN: Print 978-1-62315-639-8 | eBook 978-1-62315-641-1

CONTENTS

INTRODUCTION

WHY I RUN

"Success isn't how far you got, but the distance you traveled from where you started."

STEVE PREFONTAINE, OLYMPIC RUNNER

WHEN I JOINED THE CROSS-COUNTRY TEAM ON A WHIM IN EIGHTH GRADE, I had no idea running would become a major part of my life. I ran track and cross-country all four years of high school, and I would occasionally run a few miles around campus in college, but if you had told me that this would become a daily ritual for decades to come, I would have laughed at you. It was just something I did without thinking much about it.

And then, during my junior year of college, my mom passed away from breast cancer. After that, I stopped running completely. I just couldn't make my legs move anymore. I'd try to go out for a run, only to give up, walk home, and shove my running shoes into the back of my closet. I felt like I couldn't do any of the things that made me happy when she was alive. I thought I'd never run again.

A few years later I began coaching a high-school cross-country program. At one of the first meets I attended, just as the starting pistol went off to begin the race, I suddenly felt tears streaming down my cheeks. I wiped them away in shock—I'm not usually the type of person who cries in public. But I knew in that moment that something had come over me. I remembered how much I loved running and realized how much I missed it. When I got home that night, I dug my shoes out of the back of my closet and went out to try running again.

At first, it was only a mile or two, but as I started running more consistently again, things gradually fell back into place. I was happier. I was more creative. I felt better about myself, and I became a better friend and family member. I was myself again.

Since then, I've continued to run and challenge myself. I ran my first marathon, and then I ran twelve more. I switched up my training and strove to reclaim the strength and speed I had in high school. Finally, after training for a long time, I did something I'd never thought possible: I qualified for the Boston Marathon.

Many people give up on running before they even try it. They think of it as that chore they had to do as punishment back when they were on a sports team, or they just assume it'll be too hard. I want to change people's minds about running. Give running a chance. You may be surprised how much you love it.

Coaching has given me a new outlook on running. I love encouraging people to embrace it, no matter what level they're at. With this book, I want to encourage women who have never run before to take their first steps. It's easy to get caught up in worrying about how you look, how fast you run, your performance in a race, or whether or not you enter a race at all, but running is so much more than that. It's a personal journey. It can take you to amazing, unknown places. No matter when, where, why, or how you're running, it's something you do for *you.*

Throughout this book, you'll find nuggets of information, motivation, and helpful tips to make running a part of your lifestyle, no matter where you are along your running journey. Just remember to keep a positive mindset and enjoy each and every step.

1
RUNNING FOR LIFE

"Running is the greatest metaphor for life, because you get out of it what you put into it."

OPRAH WINFREY

Run with Benefits

Between work and family, we're all busy these days, and it can be easy to think of running as an extravagance you just don't have time for. But when you make a daily habit of running, the benefits become a powerful, indescribable force in your life—not a time suck at all. There are some very specific reasons why running is worth every minute; not only does it feel good, but it can also have a positive effect on many aspects of your life.

EMOTIONAL SUPPORT

Emotionally, running provides a great distraction-free environment to help you sort out thoughts and feelings. Whether you're dealing with family issues, work gripes, or drama with friends, the act of running gives you a chance to reflect on situations that you wouldn't normally have the opportunity to dissect. You may end up looking at certain parts of your life in a whole new way.

SHAPING UP

One benefit of running is that it keeps all the muscles in your body in shape, including the most important one: the heart. Bringing down your resting heart rate by running is great for your blood pressure and can even help you sleep better at night. Running also increases oxygen flow to your brain, keeping you sharp. Plus, running can increase your endurance, stamina, and strength, making you an overall healthier person. It's one of the best ways to get and stay fit, all while exploring your surroundings.

SELF-DISCIPLINE

Did you know that, when hiring, many companies seek out candidates who run regularly? Runners are known to have a unique sense of self-discipline, dedicating themselves to a daily practice that improves their health and overall performance. Being a runner makes you the kind of person who can get through and even enjoy a challenge, because you know how to look ahead and remind yourself of the rewards you'll reap.

"YOU" TIME

When you're out running, it's just you and the pavement. Whether you listen to music or quietly take in your surroundings, you get a special stretch of "you" time that many people hardly ever get to carve out.

WHEN YOU BEGIN TO RUN REGULARLY, YOU MAY EXPERIENCE SOME OR ALL OF THE FOLLOWING BENEFITS IN YOUR DAY-TO-DAY LIFE:

First Steps

Running is a simple sport. All you need is workout clothes, the right shoes, a little bit of time, and the outdoors. Step outside, put one foot in front of the other, and just go. If you need to walk at first, don't worry—that's completely normal. Just like with anything new, you have to start somewhere, and starting is more than half the battle. Once you start running, remember to give yourself time to adjust to how your body is feeling and take care of little aches and pains. It's okay if running is hard. It'll get easier as you adjust to your new routine and learn more about taking care of your body.

No Excuses

One of the most difficult things about running is figuring out how to fit it into your already packed schedule. Consistency is very important, especially in the beginning. You want to create a habit so that continuing to run gets easier, now and in the future.

Start by deciding which days work best for you. It could be two days a week, or it could be five—just pick something that's reasonable for you and your lifestyle. You don't want to set yourself up for failure from the beginning. Once you've chosen your days, stick to the schedule. Your body and mind will get used to the routine and eventually come to enjoy it.

If your days are already jam-packed, figure out where you have an extra hour or two to spare. Do you spend an hour sitting in traffic during your daily commute? Instead of sitting in traffic, stop by a park and run before heading home. You'll miss the worst of rush hour, enjoy exploring a new area, and, of course, get your run in for the day. If you keep a small tote with running clothes and shoes in your car, you can take a quick run on your lunch break or pull over if you see a great place to put in a few miles. You never know when that tote bag will come in handy. It could be the key to an unexpected running adventure!

If you usually spend that spare hour watching TV or straightening up the house, running might make you feel like you're "cheating" yourself out of that activity. But it's important to not look at running that way. Instead, see what you can do to make the time you spend running productive. If you run in the morning, you can use that time to mentally review the tasks ahead of you and figure out how to prioritize and organize them. If you're an evening runner, you can go over what you accomplished throughout the day and what you need to do tomorrow. With a phone or mp3 player, you can listen to a podcast or audiobook and accomplish two things at once. If you want to be extra productive, check out self-development podcasts or motivational audiobooks, which can be enriching and helpful to you in many areas of life.

Whatever you do, don't think of running as a chore or task. Think of it as taking time for yourself. You're doing something amazing—taking charge of your life and making a positive change for yourself and for your health. When you think of it that way, it becomes much easier to fit it into your schedule.

WHY DO YOU RUN?

Write down 10 specific reasons why you're beginning to run or already love to run. Is it because of the physical benefits? The runner's high? The alone time? No matter what your reasoning may be, remember that you are running for *you*. When you're struggling to get out the door, look at this list to help keep yourself motivated. Keep it in a place where you'll see it, like your closet door or by your running gear. It can help remind you of the great feelings running gives you. One of the hardest parts of running is getting started, so once you lace up your sneakers and head out the door, remind yourself that the hardest part is already over.

After a run, you will feel happy, energetic, and refreshed. ❱ *Since running increases your metabolism, you'll burn more calories throughout the day, even when you're*

HOW DO YOU MANAGE RUNNING WITH A BUSY LIFESTYLE?

Shannon Tavera

Not long ago, each run that I embarked on was calculated and predetermined. I cringed at the thought of a workout that was less than 3 miles, and my routes were spiced up with stairs and trails. Nowadays, I'll settle for a half-mile run to the nearest park, and my courses must be fit for a double-wide stroller. As a mom of two toddlers, ages one and two, and the wife of a husband with a unique work schedule, my life has become more of a balancing act than ever. My present-day running requires that I accommodate my children and rely on the support of my family.

More often than not, my only option for a run is to make it kid-friendly. Prior to departure, I stock the stroller with sippy cups and snack containers. I map out routes that will take us past fire stations, horses, water fountains, and other sights that will appeal to the eyes of toddlers. As out of breath as I may be, I prepare myself to be a tour guide on foot, pointing out a full moon, a cloud shaped like Mickey Mouse, a lizard on the sidewalk, or anything else that might serve as a quick distraction. An exciting destination, such as the park, Nana and Papa's house, or even the ice-cream shop, is a great incentive for my kids to sit a bit more patiently. On days when my kids cannot sit still for more than ten minutes at a time, I resort to literally running one errand at a time throughout the day.

At least once a week, the encouragement of a family member allows me to run with a more specific and structured purpose. Those close to me know that running makes me happy and more pleasant to be around. More than anyone else, my mom and my husband know that my entire family benefits from my running. Therefore, my mom will occasionally pick up my kids on her way home from work so I can do a speed workout on the track or lift weights at the gym. On a day home from the fire station, my husband will hold down the fort so I can tackle my long run for the week. It has become so important to be surrounded by people who realize that running is much more than exercise to me.

The bottom line is that running is a priority in my life. No matter how busy I am, I make time for it. Although running with my kids may not always be ideal, I need to remember that this is a small window of opportunity to share my love of running with them. And I find myself looking forward to a long, quiet run or a tough workout on the track.

not running. ❱ You will have a clearer mind and more focus at work. ❱ You will meet new people and expand your social circle. ❱ You will inspire those around . . .

RUNNING FOR LIFE **13**

A Lifelong Love

You may not expect to fall in love with running when you first begin, but as your relationship with it develops, it can become a lifelong companion. You may turn to running to help get you through different phases in your life, or you might find that when you have a problem and go for a run, you come back with a solution.

Running can be stressful when you're working toward a certain goal and things aren't as easy as you hoped they'd be. It can be frustrating when you're injured and have to take time off to recover. It can be disappointing if a "dream race" doesn't go as planned. In short, running can be hard at times, and every runner goes through rough patches.

RUNNER'S HIGH

When you come home from a run, you may feel refreshed, recharged, and ready to tackle tasks you were dreading. This feeling is called "runner's high," and it happens because of the endorphins your body releases when you exercise. You may not get a runner's high every single time you go for a run, but it's a feeling you'll start to crave each time you lace up your shoes. Whenever you find yourself trying to put off running, remember how good those endorphins will make you feel.

But running can also bring you incredible joy, clarity, and peace, and in the end, rough patches only make the good runs that much more memorable and special. Running offers relief from the daily grind and releases endorphins that make you happier. You may even find that running makes you a better person—calmer, clearer, and more committed and able to handle difficult situations with poise and grace. Sometimes, after a stressful day when everything seems to be going wrong, a run is the thing that will bring you home in a stronger, more positive state of mind.

YOUR CHEERING SECTION

When you're starting anything new, it's important to get the support of your family and friends. You may be surprised to find out how excited they are for you. If they run themselves, they might even give you tips or suggest some interesting routes for you to explore.

Let them know the best way to be involved in your running. Maybe they can check in with you a few times a week or hang back and let you figure out what works best for you while starting your new routine. If you're training for a race, let them know about your goals and invite them to come cheer you on. Friends and family can help keep you motivated and accountable. Just make sure you communicate what level of involvement will benefit you the most.

. . . you through your new active lifestyle. 》 *You will enjoy increased overall stamina and energy levels.* 》 *You will feel more in tune with your feelings and emotions.*

RUN WITH FRIENDS

Whether you're a seasoned pro or a beginner, running with a group can be extremely beneficial. First and foremost, a running group keeps you accountable. It's harder to back out of a run at the last minute when you know other people will notice your absence. A running group can also make running more enjoyable. Chatting with a friend as you run can help make the miles go by much faster. A running group also offers extra safety and the chance to talk about running with like-minded people. You and other members of your group may be able to share insights about running with one another, or train toward certain race goals together. And in any group, people will be running at different paces, so you can find someone to run with no matter what level you're at. If you're nervous about running in a large group, you can always ease into it. Try running with a friend and see if you enjoy it.

If you want to connect with new running buddies, visit a local running store to see if they offer an evening group run you can join. Even if they don't, they can probably point you toward other local groups. You can also find groups on different websites and forums online. Check out Meetup.com and RunnersWorld.com to find training groups and other people looking for running partners.

❯ If you start with a morning run, you'll feel more awake throughout the entire day. ❯ You will experience a sense of accomplishment after each run.

2
FIND YOUR STRIDE

"In running, it doesn't matter whether you come in first, in the middle of the pack, or last. You can say, 'I have finished.' There is a lot of satisfaction in that."

FRED LEBOW, NEW YORK CITY MARATHON COFOUNDER

The Form You Take

Everyone runs differently. Your form depends on many different factors, including your age, experience, fitness level, and body type. When you first start running, it's important to focus on completing your run instead of trying to change the mechanics of the way you run. Don't get caught up in comparing yourself to others, because the only person you're running for is yourself. And don't get discouraged by people who seem to run perfectly, because you're still new at this. Be proud of the steps you've taken to start running.

IMPROVING YOUR FORM

After you've been running regularly for a while, you'll start to feel comfortable experimenting with your form. With proper form, you can increase your speed and become a more efficient runner. It'll also be easier to avoid injury and run faster during a race.

AVOIDING INJURIES & FINISHING STRONG

Proper form helps you avoid injuries by streamlining your body's mechanics. Instead of stressing out your knees with a suboptimal foot strike or wasting energy on unnecessary movements, you'll be moving forward efficiently and learning how to push your body farther and faster.

If you run a race, proper form will help you hit the finish line feeling strong. Even though your legs and lungs will get tired, your body will be able to tap into the strength you've built up with good form and will use it to propel you across the finish line.

PERFECTING YOUR FORM

One of the best ways to capture your current running form is to have someone videotape you. Make one video that shows you running toward the camera and another that shows you running from the side. That way you can see how you currently run and figure out what you may want to change or work on.

When you start improving your form, be careful and go slow. If your body isn't prepared to make a huge change suddenly, you can end up getting injured. Also, if you're already feeling great and running injury-free, you may not need to worry about your form at all.

---

10 TIPS TO ACHIEVING GOOD FORM: *If your knees hurt on either the outside or inside your foot strike may be overpronated or oversupinated (see page 27).*

YOUR RUNNING HEART RATE

Like any activity, running will increase your heart rate. This is completely normal—in fact, it's healthy. But you don't want to push it too hard, especially in the beginning, or you may burn out too quickly. Find your average heart rate while running so you can gauge your effort and make sure you're doing what's right for your body.

To find a rough estimate of your maximum heart rate, subtract your age from 220. To find your resting heart rate, take your pulse for 60 seconds right when you wake up. Now you can figure out your recommended average running heart rate by subtracting your resting heart rate from your maximum heart rate.

The American Heart Association's heart-rate chart offers a great baseline for beginning runners. It uses the rough "220 minus age" formula I've used above, but it specifies that when you exercise, you want your heart rate to be at about 50 to 85 percent of your max heart rate. You don't want to go too much higher or lower than that target zone; if it's too high, you may overexert yourself, and if it's too low, you're not getting a challenging workout.

Remember, everyone has a different fitness level, and consistent monitoring will help you find the average that is right for you. Think about your age, the level you're running at, and your overall fitness, and don't get discouraged when you take your heart rate. Soon it'll be easier to run faster and farther, and your heart rate will be right where you want it.

Make sure you have supportive shoes to help keep your feet more stable. ❯ To prevent tension from building up in your shoulders, keep them relaxed and . . .

The Perfect Form

Here are a few tips for improving your form from two experts at the Boulder Center for Sports Medicine: Adam St. Pierre, an exercise physiologist, and Christy Barth, a physical therapist and strength-and-conditioning specialist.

Maintain a short, quick, natural stride—like you're walking, but at a faster pace. It can be tempting to "overstride," or take large steps where you reach forward with your foot. Don't do it! Overstriding can lead to tight muscles throughout your legs and arch problems in your foot.

Keep your knees in line with your feet. Make sure your foot strikes the ground under your knee, not in front of it, or you could end up with injured knees. This is especially important when running downhill.

Don't drag your feet. Instead, focus on pushing up and off the ground behind you while also being light on your feet. Listen to your shoes when they hit the ground. They shouldn't make a loud noise or sound like they are dragging or shuffling. In fact, they should hardly make any noise at all.

ARMS & HANDS

Many people struggle with their arms and hands when running—what are you supposed to do with them, anyway? First, relax your hands into natural, loose fists. It helps to imagine that you have a potato chip between the tips of your middle finger and thumb. Keep your hands at your sides, below your heart, and try not to punch them forward or cross them in front of your chest. Your elbows should be bent at 90 degrees or less.

JUST BREATHE

You already know how to breathe. But do you know the right way to breathe while you're running?

Always breathe through your mouth when you're running—breathing through your nose alone won't give you as much oxygen as you need. Breathe long and slow and deep, all the way down to the bottom of your lungs.

If you get short of breath, don't try to breathe in more. Instead, try breathing out more. You want to empty your lungs all the way down to the bottom so you can fill them back up again on the next breath.

When you're running, try to match your breathing to your steps. I like to breathe in for three steps, and then breathe out for four steps. Find whatever pattern works for you. The more you run, the more you'll understand your own rhythms, and breathing is a big part of that.

... take deep breaths while you're running. ❯ Don't clench your fists when you run. It takes up energy that you could be using for running. ❯ If your new shoes are

Try to be cognizant of your shoulders. As you get tired, your shoulders will likely tighten and become tense, and you may start pulling them up around your neck without realizing it. If that happens, let your arms fall to your sides and shake them out. Check your shoulders every now and then to see if they're creeping up: if they are, relax them. When you run longer distances, try to push your shoulders back and your chest out. This will keep your shoulders from curling inward and then becoming sore the next day.

When you're running, look ahead of you, not down. This clues you in to your surroundings and keeps your neck straight and posture upright. You might find yourself looking downward on instinct, because naturally you don't want to step on anything or twist your ankle, but as you gain more experience, you'll become more confident and sure-footed and you won't feel the need to look down as much.

IMPROVING YOUR CORE

It's often overlooked, but having a strong core is an essential part of running. A strong core promotes good posture and prevents you from hunching over when you get tired.

Sit-ups, push-ups, planks, and leg lifts can make a huge difference to your core muscles and your running form. Try to add in a short core workout after each run to maximize your routine (see page 50). It doesn't have to be long. Even a five-minute core workout makes a difference. You can even do repetitions between stretches after a run.

hurting your feet, give them some time to get "broken in" and mold to your foot before you attempt a longer run. ❳ *When you have a bad run, take time to . . .*

Other Ways to Run

BAREFOOT RUNNING

The art of running is constantly evolving, and with that evolution come new ideas about alternate running forms. One popular alternate form is the barefoot method, also known as natural running, which is when you run with very minimal shoes or no shoes at all. It's a controversial practice, and scientific research hasn't reached a clear consensus about its risks or its benefits.

Many people who try it are used to running in shoes, and when they try to make the transition to barefoot running, they do it too quickly and get injured. But practiced barefoot runners often claim that shoes actually increase injuries, because human beings didn't evolve to run in them. They believe that once you get used to it, running barefoot makes you a more efficient runner and helps with your form, because it's how the body was naturally meant to run.

The recent interest in natural running has led many runners to try out thin-soled and flexible shoes, like Vibram FiveFingers and Merrell Bareforms. More traditional moccasins and huaraches have also entered the running-shoe market.

CHI RUNNING

Another popular alternate form of running is ChiRunning, which aims to be a gentle but powerful way to minimize injuries or come back from an injury stronger than ever. This method blends movement principles from the Chinese martial art *t'ai chi ch'uan* with the active movement of running to create a more mindful, centered, and balanced approach to the sport.

The foundations of ChiRunning are good posture and proper biomechanics. ChiRunning coaches work with runners on their form, helping them figure out why their injuries are happening and how to eliminate them. They emphasize using core muscles, which are stronger and more efficient than heavy leg muscles. ChiRunners also learn how to engage gravity, so that their legs aren't doing more work than they have to. As their motto says, "It ain't the muscle, it's the motion."

> **The will to win means nothing without the will to prepare.**
>
> JUMA IKANGAA,
> 1989 NYC MARATHON WINNER

. . . evaluate what went wrong and remind yourself that tomorrow will be better. ❯ *Cool down properly and stretch after each run to keep lactic acid from building up*

22 RUNNING FOR WOMEN

HOW DID YOU FIND YOUR STRIDE?

Glennis Seldon

I have been running for more than 20 years. I started running at the early age of seven. One of the first things I was taught was how to properly swing my arms so that I would be a more efficient runner. My club track coach would yell out "L . . . V . . . L . . . V" as we walked 50 meters swinging our arms trying to make our arms look like an L and a V. We would also sit on the ground doing the same thing. He would say "the faster your arms move, the faster you run." I would do my best to remember the drill while I was running.

When I got to high school my form started to get a little sloppy. Although I was our top varsity cross-country and distance track runner, I struggled with keeping my shoulders down and not swinging my arms across my chest. I can still hear my coach yelling, "Relax your shoulders!" He would tell me when you drop your shoulders and swing your arms back and forth you will run faster. It was a challenge remembering this while running. Sometimes I would feel myself getting tired and shoulders would creep up, and I would remind myself to take a deep breath in and exhale. I would relax, and my form would be better.

By the time I got to college, I was still running the same. My college coach would have me do the LV drill with weights. I would stand in a running position looking at myself in the mirror with a five- to ten-pound dumb-bell in each hand and swing my arms back and forth for 30 secs as fast as I could. This drill really helped because it forced me to keep my shoulders relaxed and not swing my arms across my body so much.

Now that I am an elite runner my form is so much better! My current coach taught me some drills that I do about two to three times a week that have helped improve my running form. One of my favorites is called over-exaggerated strides. This is where you run about 50 meters at 50-60% speed while swinging your arms big and lifting your knees. You want your hands to go past your head and past your hips making sure your elbows don't stick out. Bring your knees up, keeping your feet flexed so that you are landing on the balls of your feet. In a race, when you are tired at the end and feel like you can't go on anymore, you can think about over-exaggerating with big movements of your arms and legs and in reality they will be perfect.

Everything that I have learned over the years has made me a better runner. Having great form can make a huge difference in a race. Everyone is tired at the end of the race, but whoever has the best form often is the one who wins. This is why your form is so important; it could be the difference between a gold medal and a silver medal, a personal record or a season's best. Practice and be patient.

in your muscles and causing soreness. ❱ *Don't let your period stop you from running. Try tampons that are made specifically for athletic activities.* ❱

Always Running

DURING YOUR PERIOD

Your period can put a damper on your motivation and your running routine. When you're menstruating or about to start, you can feel bloated and lethargic, and it's very easy to talk yourself out of going for a run. However, don't doubt your ability! It may be a bit harder to get started, but you'll feel much better once you're out the door.

In fact, many women who run during this time report that it boosts their energy and mood and helps with back pain and overall soreness. Running increases blood flow throughout your body and releases endorphins, which can help you feel invigorated. It also helps with bloating, because it passes gas through the digestive tract, relieving pressure. Of course, if you're dealing with severe cramping or PMS symptoms, you can always take a day or two off until you feel comfortable running again.

When running during your period, use the menstrual products that make you feel the most comfortable. It's generally easier to run with a tampon (or menstrual cup) than with a traditional pad, but the choice is up to you.

If you want, keep a running journal to see how your cycle affects your training plan. Jot down how you feel after each run, and track when your period comes each month. Some women experience great running in the days before they start to menstruate, while others have the opposite experience and find that it's a bit of a struggle. Others don't notice much

of a difference at all. Regardless, keeping track of how your body works will help you create the personalized training plan that's best for you.

WHILE PREGNANT

If and how you run during pregnancy is a very personal decision, and there are a lot of factors to take into account. Personally, when I got pregnant, I imagined I would stick to my normal routine and run more or less the same throughout my pregnancy as I always did. Nope! I was sidelined from the beginning, because I just didn't feel good enough to run.

Here are a couple of tips that you may find helpful if you're running while pregnant: Always remember that pregnancy is different for everyone. What works for some people may not work for you, and that's okay. It's easy to drive yourself crazy looking on the Internet to find out what everyone else is doing, but you should confer with your doctor and then do what feels best for you. Remind yourself daily that you're healthy and that your body is doing one of the most amazing things a body can do. Don't push yourself. If something feels off, stop immediately. It's not worth it to keep running just for the sake of running. Now is the most important time to listen to your body. If you feel uncomfortable, don't focus on increasing your distance or improving your pace. Leave the watch at home and just run based on how you feel.

When you're pregnant, it's important to surround yourself with people who support you. Some people may question why you're still running if they personally think it's not

---

If you're pregnant and running is becoming hard for you, try using a support belt. It'll help brace your growing belly as you run. 〉 *Are you in a running slump?*

safe, but it's important to do what you and your doctor have established is right for you. If you do decide it's time to take a break, try to find another outlet that brings you joy. It can be discouraging to press "pause" on running when it's a big part of your life, but just think of all the good things to come—including your tiny new running partner!

WITH A STROLLER

Regular strollers aren't made to take on a run. If you want to bring your baby on a run with you, you'll want to look into running or jogging strollers.

The wheels on a jogging stroller are bigger than those on a normal stroller, with extra large rear wheels to navigate bumps in the road. The tires are filled with air, which reduces the impact of any turbulence on your baby and gives you less resistance as you push the stroller forward. A locking front

wheel keeps the stroller steady, so it doesn't wobble as you increase your speed. (If a wobbly front wheel hits a bump and turns sharply, the stroller could tip over, which would be a very dangerous situation.)

Unlike a normal stroller, a jogging stroller also has a suspension system and a reclined seat, so your child can enjoy a safer, smoother ride without the stress from bumpy terrain traveling straight up his or her spine. These features work so well that many babies even fall asleep in running strollers.

A quick note: Even with a jogging stroller, running can put stress on babies who aren't yet old enough to hold their heads up. Check with your pediatrician to see if your baby's neck muscles are strong enough for the jogging stroller. Once you get the thumbs up, there are plenty of models out there that'll let your new running partner relax and enjoy the ride as you run.

Take a week-long break and head back out on your own terms, when you feel ready. If you're having back problems while running, you may have a . . .

Go For a Run

Now that you've learned about form, it's time to put a few things into practice and go for a run. Start with a warm up of five to seven minutes. Relax, and run at a slower pace than you normally would. Do a few stretches to warm up your legs, including toe touches, deep lunges, and leg swings on a nearby stationary object.

Then head out for your run. Keep your run on the shorter side, and don't worry about speed or pace. While you're running, think about your form. Do you catch yourself over-striding or hunching up your shoulders? Now that you've read this chapter, you may notice

problems you'd overlooked before and now want to change. That's fantastic, but remember to stay relaxed and don't overthink it. Too much change at once can cause injuries.

Once you return from your run, cool down for five minutes or so to relax your muscles and bring your heart rate back to normal. Just as you did in your warm up, run slower than normal. And of course, don't forget to stretch. If you don't stretch, your muscles can tighten up, which can lead to injuries. Start with toe touches and deep lunges, and make sure you really stretch out your hamstrings and quads. Don't neglect your arms and back—they've helped carry your body through the run, too!

After you finish stretching, it's time for core work. Do three sets of 15 push-ups and sit-ups, and then finish by planking for a minute (see page 51). Don't worry if you can't do a minute-long plank right off the bat. Just work on increasing the duration each time you plank. As your core gets stronger, these exercises will get easier.

LIKE A FINE WINE, RUNNING GETS BETTER WITH AGE

Unlike many other female athletes, women who run tend to peak in performance as they age. Maybe it's because they're more relaxed and better able to clear their minds or they just know what they want, but many women report having more euphoric running experiences as they get older. As long as you take care of yourself and tend to any injuries, you're doing your body a huge favor by committing to a regular running routine. You're working to stay healthy, and you'll reap the rewards as you continue to run throughout your life.

. . . pinched nerve. Schedule a visit to your local chiropractor.

THE SOLE SEARCH: What You Need To Know About Feet

All runners have different feet, and if you want to perfect your stride, it's important to know what kind of feet you're working with and how they hit the ground. A great way to learn what type of foot strike you have is to dip your foot in water, take a normal step, and look at your footprint. You'll be able to see what your arch is like, which side of your foot your weight is falling on, and whether you're flat-footed.

If your wet footprint has a slight arch and all the parts of the foot visible, you have a neutral or "normal" foot strike. When you take a step, the outside part of your heel touches the ground first, and then the rest of the foot follows, coming in complete contact with the surface. At the end of the step, you should push off evenly from the front of the foot to propel yourself forward.

If your wet footprint shows your entire foot with no definite arch, your foot strike is over-pronated. This means that your ankles roll inward when you take a step. In an overpronated foot strike, the outer edge of the heel touches the ground first, and then the foot rolls inward and flattens out. Excessive overpronation can injure your ankles and knees.

If your wet footprint makes it look like barely any of your mid-foot touches the ground at all or like you have an extremely high arch, your foot strike is oversupinated. Oversupination is the opposite of overpronation—the foot rolls outward during normal motion, not inward. Oversupination puts a lot of strain on the muscles and tendons that stabilize the ankle, and in some cases it can cause you to sprain your ankle or tear your ligaments. Another reason to use good running form!

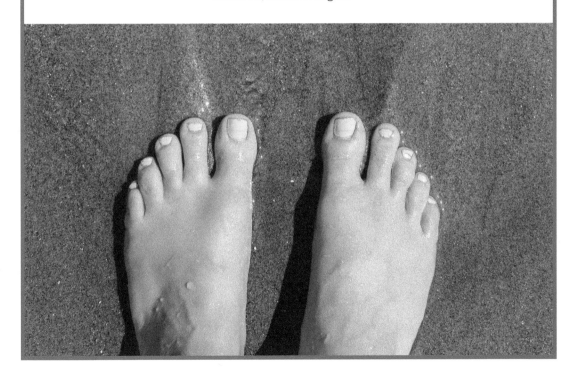

3

GEAR
& SAFETY

"Running should be a lifelong activity. Approach it patiently and intelligently, and it will reward you for a long, long time."

MICHAEL SARGENT

Run Safe

Every day, millions of people around the world put on their shoes, open the front door, and head out for a run. For most, everything will go smoothly. But every so often, problems do happen. Whether you're a beginner or an old pro, there are health and safety hazards to be aware of while you're running. The more you know about these potential problems, the better you can prepare for them and make sure your run is safe, fun, and healthy.

The first and most important rule to stay safe while running: Be aware of your surroundings at all times. This is especially imperative when it comes to running in high-traffic areas—even a minor driving error can have severe consequences for a runner who isn't paying attention. You should also be mindful of nature and wildlife (and not-so-wildlife, including neighborhood dogs). Is it sunny, rainy, or windy? Weather conditions can make a big impact on your run. The time of day makes a difference, too. If you're running at dusk or dawn, the dim lighting makes it harder for you to see your surroundings and for others to see you. If you go running after dark, take special care to make yourself visible and stay alert to your environment.

In addition to these possible safety risks, running can be physically difficult. Always prioritize your health and wellness. Of course, it's rare for a medical emergency to pop up during a run, but it does happen, and it's much better to be safe than sorry. Running with your cell phone is a good idea if you can manage it.

These are all commonsense safety guidelines. Don't let fear of the unknown stop you from getting out there and running! With the proper accessories and mindset, you can safely enjoy your run, no matter where or when you do it.

JOGGING AT NIGHT

Nighttime running can be invigorating—but also a little scary, so you want to be prepared for anything.

Invest in a headlamp so you can see the sidewalk and avoid falling and injuring yourself. Wear reflective gear and blinking lights, as drivers are scurrying home after work or dinner and may not be paying enough attention to their surroundings. Look both ways and proceed with caution when you cross any kind of driveway.

It is very unlikely that you'll be attacked, but you can always carry pepper spray with you to be extra safe. I advise bringing your phone, too, just in case something does happen. You can even download apps that will send alerts to a selected person if you press an emergency button on your phone. If you still don't feel secure running at night, don't run.

Above all, try to run in a well-lit area, and make sure someone knows where you are and when you expect to return.

THE FOLLOWING GUIDELINES WILL HELP YOU GEAR UP AND STAY SAFE AS YOU EMBARK ON YOUR NEW RUNNING JOURNEY: *Make sure your shoes . . .*

Essential Running Gear

High-quality gear can make all the difference between a good run and a bad one, and the single most important piece of running equipment is a solid pair of running shoes. You can always run in cotton shirts and old gym shorts, but if your shoes are worn out, improperly fitted, or otherwise subpar, you could experience discomfort or injury that can sideline you for months.

The best place to find the right shoe—or any type of gear—is at a local running store. Bigger sports chains can be great, but their employees may not have the expertise to help you find the proper shoe. The people who work at smaller, local running stores tend to be runners themselves, so they're usually the best resource for finding reliable gear. Don't be afraid to ask questions about the products you're trying out, especially shoes. Good sales associates may look closely at your arches or ask you to run for them so they can see your stride.

It's absolutely essential to keep your feet healthy when you're running. They're what hits the pavement over and over, so they do a lot of work and undergo a lot of stress. The right shoes can help you prevent calluses, ingrown toenails, and blisters, along with more serious injuries like tendonitis and plantar fasciitis. The better your feet feel, the better your run will be.

The same goes for your legs! They do the hard work of propelling you forward, so you want to make sure they're always feeling fresh and ready for your next run. To keep your legs in tip-top shape, do a lot of icing, stretching, and foam rolling.

And don't forget about your hips, your lungs, and your skin—when you're running, your whole body is a machine. You need to maintain it well with the right gear and a lot of care. Make an appointment with your doctor, get a heart-rate monitor, buy a new pair of shoes—whatever you need to do to listen to and take care of your body.

SHOES

Many people pick shoes based on looks, but that is a terrible idea. The cutest shoes in the world are worthless if they make running harder or more painful than it should be. I've seen too many people get injuries just from buying the wrong shoe, so take the time to find the right one. It can make a huge difference.

The right shoe for you is one that fits *your* foot, so doing online research for the "best running shoe" won't help. It's all about your personal foot arch, your stride, and the type of cushioning you need. I need a neutral shoe, for example, with a wide toe box and a bit of extra cushioning. I've found that the extra cushioning helps me a lot during long runs, plus the shoes last longer.

Keep in mind that proper running shoes can be expensive, anywhere from $100 to $175, depending on the brand. Look for a trusted brand instead of a knockoff from a mass retailer like Target, Payless, or Walmart; their running shoes are not made for long distances and can break down very quickly, which is a surefire way to get injuries.

Remember that your feet will likely swell when running. This is completely natural. You may want to buy running shoes a half or full size bigger than usual, so your feet have room to expand a bit without giving you blisters.

SPORTS BRAS

Running is a high-impact activity, which means you're in for a lot of bouncing. Luckily, there's a wide array of sports bras with many different features to help you minimize breast movement. It's important to get the correct support for your breasts when running, because once you stretch out the ligaments that hold the breasts up, they don't unstretch. This can create sagging and back problems.

When you're in the market for a new sports bra, start by looking at the band that sits around your midsection under your breasts. It provides the majority of the bra's support, and the wider it is, the better. Wider straps work the same way. Just make sure they won't slip off or dig into your shoulders.

There are three main styles of sports bras: compression, encapsulation, and a hybrid of compression and encapsulation.

COMPRESSION BRAS are a better fit for those with a smaller bust. They compress the breasts against the chest to limit movement. For maximum support, try the racerback style.

If you're bustier, go for the **ENCAPSULATION BRA**. Instead of compressing the breasts, it uses individual cups to support and surround each breast separately. These bras also usually have underwire, which can provide extra support and shape.

The **HYBRID BRA**, halfway between compression and encapsulation, works better if you have a larger bust. It combines the compression feature with individual cups for each breast.

. . . *allow enough room for your feet to swell.* ❯ *Moisture-wicking socks can help alleviate blisters.* ❯ *Invest in ice packs that mold to your body so you can easily put*

32 RUNNING FOR WOMEN

k, and drivers in a ot be aware of their gs. Always make : with drivers when e street in front of e have been many n I very well might hit if I didn't make ct with a driver and to acknowledge my . Wear your reflec- in the mornings to your visibility.

If you're running in a wilder area, be aware of animals like coyotes or mountain lions that are active at dawn and dusk. They're mostly scared of humans, but you should know your plan in the unlikely event that one approaches you.

It's a great idea to greet fellow runners and walkers with a friendly hello and wave. You never know when they may need your help or vice versa.

them on any sore muscle. 》 During inclement weather, make sure to wear layers instead of bulking up on heavy clothes. 》 Body Glide can help with chafing . . .

If you can, try to find a bra that isn't made of cotton—you'll experience less chafing that way. Wicking fabrics are best, because they help keep you comfortable even when you sweat, although you may find your fabric options limited, especially with sturdier bras. As running becomes more popular, there are a lot of companies improving their sports bra selections. Some great brands to check out are Moving Comfort, Athleta, and Zensah.

SHORTS, PANTS, AND SKIRTS

With so many companies offering running clothes these days, you have almost limitless options. You can spring for high-end options or get something more affordable at places like Target, Walmart, or TJ Maxx. There are near-endless colors, designs, and features, so have fun with it! There's no right or wrong thing to wear, and picking out new clothes can make you excited to go running.

The bottom half of your running attire can come in many different fabrics. Spandex is one of the most common materials, but it's by no means necessary. For some people, spandex can minimize chafing, but for others, it can make chafing worse. No matter what you choose to run in, check if the material is moisture-wicking, so you can stay dry and avoid sweat-related discomfort. Cotton can be a good option for a short run, but because it's not moisture wicking, it may get uncomfortable as your mileage increases. Be aware that your body will heat up as you run. You may want to opt for shorts instead of pants, even if it's cold out, so you won't overheat later on.

> " If you want to become the best runner you can be, start now. Don't spend the rest of your life wondering if you can do it. "
>
> PRISCILLA WELCH, MARATHON RUNNER

One of the newest pieces of attire to hit the market is a running skirt, with or without built-in shorts. They make many women feel empowered—there's nothing like the feeling of passing a man during a race while wearing a skirt. Check out RunningSkirts.com and SparkleAthletic.com for great running skirts.

SHIRTS & TANK TOPS

You'll find a huge selection of shirts and tank tops at any sports store, and most of them are great. A cotton shirt is fine for a short, cool-weather run, but during a humid five-miler, you'll probably want a moisture-wicking fabric to prevent chafing. Don't worry about the price—a $10 shirt works just as well as a $75 shirt if they're made of the same material. When you get a new shirt, take it out for a shorter test run, just to make sure that it fits well and is comfortable. Pay special attention to the sleeves; ill-fitting seams or baggy arm-holes can cause chafing around your armpits.

. . . on the entire body—use it where you need it. 》 Always take a new item of clothing on a shorter run before putting it to the test on a long run. 》 Never wash

34 RUNNING FOR WOMEN

SAFETY ACCESSORIES

Be safe when you're out running. Always run with some form of identification on you, just in case. I recommend the Road ID, which attaches to your wrist or shoelace and displays a few lines of text that you've chosen, including pertinent medical information. In a worst-case scenario, it could help an emergency responder save your life.

Hopefully you'll never have to use it, but carrying pepper spray can effectively deter an attacker. If you wear it prominently on your wrist, a predator may think twice about coming after you. Just make sure you're familiar with how to use it before taking it out with you on a run.

If you plan on running near dawn or dusk, it's smart to wear reflective gear and/or clothing with reflective accents. You can also wear a small blinking light on your front or back or on your shoelaces. That way, drivers, bikers, and other pedestrians can see you from a distance, even in dim light, and you can avoid a collision.

SUNGLASSES

Sunglasses are more than just a fashion statement when you're out running. They keep you from having to squint, prevent bugs from flying into your eyes, and protect your eyes in general. Don't feel obligated to get the wraparound models you often see Olympians running in. I personally opt for a more fashionable frame from Oakley, and I've also had great success with Ryders. The most

ON A TREADMILL

If you're running on a treadmill instead of heading outside, there are a few things to take into consideration. First of all, make sure you're comfortable with the speed. Start at a slower pace, and then speed up gradually. Don't try to jump on at a faster speed unless you've had extensive experience with this method; you can really injure yourself that way. If you want a more intense workout at a lower speed, you can always increase the elevation of the treadmill to replicate an outdoor hill workout.

The pre-programmed workouts on a treadmill can push you to run faster or farther than you would outdoors, so feel free to challenge yourself and try one out.

Even though you're running on a treadmill, it's important to maintain your warm up and cool-down routines to help your muscles prepare for and recover from your run.

your running shoes in the washing machine. It breaks them down much faster. ⟩ If your clothes are really sweaty, avoid mildew by letting them hang dry before . . .

GEAR & SAFETY **35**

important thing when looking at any pair of sunglasses? The sticker that says, "Blocks 100% of UVA and UVB rays."

Don't be afraid to try them on for a run around the store. You want to make sure you like them and that they stay on your face when you're on the move. They should have a nosepiece to keep them from sliding down your face, and they should fit snugly but not too tightly. Trust me, you don't want too-tight frames giving you a headache while you're running—I speak from experience.

SUNSCREEN

Sunscreen is almost as important as shoes and clothes while running, even when it's not very sunny out. The sun's rays are so powerful that you can get burned even through cloud cover at eight in the morning. Make sure you apply sunscreen to all exposed areas, including the part in your hair, and consider a hat or visor to help keep the rays off the extra-delicate skin on your face.

Make sure your sunscreen is waterproof—you don't want it running into your eyes as soon as you start sweating. Stick to an SPF of 30 or higher, because you will be in the sun for an extended period of time. And don't forget a lip balm with SPF to protect your lips.

WATER BOTTLES

Hydration is important while you're running, so lots of people choose to bring a water bottle along.

The most basic and inexpensive option is the handheld water bottle, which usually consists of a plastic water bottle with a strap that goes over it so you can carry it in your hand. It may feel awkward the first few times you run with it, but you'll adjust. Just make sure to switch hands every so often so one arm doesn't get more tired than the other. These usually cost around $10 to $20.

If you want something a little more advanced, CamelBak offers a backpack-style hydration system that allows you to drink as you run through a small straw that goes over your shoulder. That way, your hands are free and the weight of the water is distributed evenly on your back. These run $20 and up.

Another option is a fuel belt, which fastens around your waist with Velcro or a clip. You place multiple smaller water bottles around the belt so that the weight of the belt is distributed evenly. Fuel belts also usually have a small pouch or pocket to put an energy bar or other "fuel" in. These normally cost around $25 and up.

. . . putting them in your hamper. ❩ *Arm warmers can be a light and functional alternative to a jacket or sweater. Try pairing them with a tank in cold weather.* ❩

Pick a Soundtrack

If you need some extra motivation while running, it's a good idea to invest in a portable music player. Whether you use your phone or a separate piece of equipment, music is a great way to make your run go by faster. Most people wear their phone or mp3 player in an armband or attach it to their clothing with a clip.

You can buy many different kinds of headphones for your music player, including wireless ones, ones that wrap around your ears, and ones that slide into your ears. Make sure they're comfortable and fit well enough to stay in your ears even when you're sweating. If you're a heavy sweater, you may want to look into waterproof headphones. Koss Earphones, Yurbuds, and Sony all make good headphones for runners.

Tracking Your Run

As more and more people start to run, more technologically advanced tools keep popping up to help you make your run more interactive and trackable. Some trackers even help keep you safe by logging your location in real time while you're out running.

I recommend tracking each run in some way, even if it's just by using a wristwatch to see how long you ran for. When you know how far and fast you just ran, you can see how you're improving, which both keeps you accountable to yourself and motivates you to keep running. Many runners choose to run with a wearable tracker or a phone with a tracking app. (A phone is great because it also makes it easy to get in contact with someone in case of an emergency.)

Compression clothing increases blood flow to sore muscles, helping them recover faster. 》 To prevent muscle tightness, invest in a foam roller to use before bed . . .

SOCIAL MEDIA SHARING & APPS

If you run with your smartphone, try out a running app like Nike+, MapMyRun, Strava, or—my personal favorite—RunKeeper. They all have different interfaces, so if you don't like the way one functions, just give another one a spin.

Many runners love to share their running activities on social media. It can be a super fun motivator to share your time, pace, and other stats with your friends, but don't feel obligated to do it if you don't want to. And do be aware that if you publicly share a map of where you ran, you might be accidentally giving strangers your home address.

WEARABLE TRACKERS

Many runners like to use wearable trackers that monitor not only their runs, but also their daily steps, calorie intake, and more. If you're looking to lose weight or just make your lifestyle a little healthier, these devices will help you by keeping a detailed diary of your routine and offering insights on your pace, mileage, and other running stats. They also give you the option to join groups. Some great brands to check out are Fitbit, Garmin, Mio, and Jawbone. Compare features online to determine which one is right for you.

ROUGH WEATHER

The weather can always change at a moment's notice, so it's important to know what to wear when running in any condition. As you gain more experience, you'll get better at picking out clothes that work for you in different types of weather.

As mentioned before, your body temperature will rise while you're running, so layers are a runner's best friends.

You can always take off a light jacket and tie it around your waist, but if you choose to wear pants and get too warm, taking them off isn't really an option.

If it's raining, less is more. Wet fabric is more likely to chafe and become uncomfortably heavy. It's no fun to have a soaked fleece pullover weighting you down as you head home in a sudden storm. Make sure your clothes are temperature-appropriate, moisture-wicking, and lightweight even when wet.

. . . or while you're watching TV. ❭ Always make sure at least one person knows where you are running and when you expect to return. ❭ If you're running in a busy

38 RUNNING FOR WOMEN

Injuries

All runners deal with injury at some point, but you can prevent most trouble with proper care and home remedies. Don't hesitate to call a doctor if the injury lingers longer than a week or if you see no improvement after a few different treatments. In addition to your general practitioner, you may need to see a specialist who can help pinpoint the problem and offer the best treatment plan. A second opinion can also be helpful. Certain injuries may require you to take time off from running, which can be frustrating to deal with. Listen to your doctor. If he or she tells you to take time off, then take time off, or you could end up hurting yourself even worse.

Prevention is the best way to keep injuries at bay. Always stretch both before and after a run, and do small activities throughout the day to help keep your body feeling good. Take those extra 3 minutes daily to stretch your calves, Achilles tendons, hamstrings, and feet, even if it means stretching against the wall at work. You can also foam roll your entire body to help with soreness and increase blood flow to your muscles (see page 48).

The most important home remedy to remember is RICE: Rest, Ice, Compression, Elevation. I remind the team I coach about this every single day. If any area of your body is feeling sore, RICE can be the key to your recovery.

HAVEN'T YOU EARNED A MASSAGE?

If you really want to treat yourself, schedule a massage as a reward for finishing a week of hard workouts or longer runs. Not only is a massage a great relaxation tool, it's also an effective way to prevent injury. It helps improve blood flow throughout the body, which positively impacts all of your different body parts. Plus, massages can help you recover faster, improve your performance, reduce your muscle soreness, and increase your flexibility with some light stretching.

Mention to your massage therapist that you're a runner, and they can focus on areas that might need extra attention, like your feet, iliotibial band (IT) band, and shoulders. They can also recommend stretches to help you release extra tightness. Remember to drink a lot of water to flush out any toxins that may be released during a massage.

area, use only one ear bud and keep your music low so you can hear your surroundings. ❯ *Need extra motivation? Add new music to your playlist before a run . . .*

TWELVE COMMON INJURIES

BLISTERS

A blister is a raised portion of skin that's filled with fluid. It is caused by friction on the skin, which can happen if your shoes are too tight or if your socks rub against your sweaty feet.

To prevent blisters, make sure your shoes fit you right, and invest in moisture-wicking socks.

Blisters can heal naturally. The unbroken skin over a blister provides a natural barrier to bacteria and decreases the risk of infection, so if you have to drain the blister, try to keep the overlying skin intact. Wash your hands beforehand, and puncture the blister near its edge with a sterilized needle. Let the fluid drain, and cover it with a bandage.

MUSCLE CRAMPS

A muscle cramp is a strong, painful contraction or tightening of the muscle that comes on suddenly and lasts for a few seconds to a few minutes. It usually happens because the muscle is dehydrated and/or overused.

To prevent muscle cramps, drink eight glasses of water daily and more on hot days. Stretch the problem muscle more during your normal routine.

If you experience a muscle cramp, immediately stop and massage the location. Try to relax and take deep breaths. If it's in your leg, you can lie down and put the leg up in the air to decrease pressure on the area that is cramping.

MUSCLE STRAIN

A muscle strain is a stretch or tear in your muscle tissue (or your tendon, which is the tissue that connects the muscles to the surrounding bones). Repetitive motion can lead to strains, and runners usually get them in their calves or hamstrings.

To prevent muscle strain, stretch properly both before and after running. Ice any tight spots to decrease inflammation.

Icing is very important when it comes to muscle strains. Place a bag of ice on the injured area for 10 minutes at a time, then take it off for 30 minutes. (Don't place the ice directly on your skin, because it can leave a burn.) Icing slows down the inflammation in a given area and eases pain and swelling.

SHIN SPLINTS

Shin splints—a general term for pain on or around the shinbone—are one of the most common running injuries. They're typically caused by irritated and swollen muscles, and they usually mean that you're not wearing the right shoes.

To prevent shin splints, get properly fitted for the right shoes, and stretch your calves throughout the day.

If you're already experiencing shin splints, ice, ice, ice! Do it for 20 minutes daily. Take ibuprofen or aspirin to help with pain and swelling. Try wearing a compression sleeve when you run to support your shins and provide pain relief.

RUNNER'S KNEE

Runner's knee is usually described as pain behind or around the kneecap. You may feel pain or even hear a popping or grinding sound when you bend your knee.

To prevent runner's knee, wear a support band on your tendon or a brace on your knee when you run. Foam rolling your IT band can help keep the tendons surrounding the knee from becoming too tight, which is often what causes runner's knee.

. . . to switch things up. 》 *To avoid headphone wires tangling while you run, invest in wireless Bluetooth headphones.* 》 *Running shoes only last for roughly*

40 RUNNING FOR WOMEN

Ice is a key component in healing runner's knee. Elevate your knee when you're seated. Take aspirin or ibuprofen 10 minutes before you leave for your run to help with swelling and pain. Continue to foam roll your IT band to help release tension in the surrounding tendons (see page 48).

SIDE STITCHES

A side stitch is a cramp or pain that occurs under the ribcage. It can be caused by dehydration or eating before running.

To prevent side stitches, try to run more on an empty stomach than a full belly. Avoid carbonated drinks before running.

If you develop a side stitch while running, try to keep going and massage or press on the area that hurts. If you need to, stop running and push your hand upward into the right side of your belly while inhaling and exhaling evenly. Try to relax and take deep breaths. Here's one strange remedy that I always use for side stiches: While running, push your belly out really far, but continue to breathe. It sounds weird, but it always seems to work!

IT BAND SORENESS

The IT band is a large ligament that runs down the outside of the thigh. If you overuse it or don't stretch it properly, you'll feel soreness and tightness on the outside of the knee or hip.

To prevent IT band soreness, stretch before and after each run, and make sure your shoes fit right to avoid overpronation.

Stretch and foam roll your IT band consistently. Foam rolling can be very painful at first, but it gets much better as you loosen up the IT band. If necessary, a physical therapist can massage the area.

PLANTAR FASCIITIS

Plantar fasciitis is the inflammation of the tissue that reaches from the heel to the toes, supporting the muscles and arch of the foot. When this tissue gets overstretched, tiny, painful tears can appear.

250 to 400 miles. Track your miles so you know when it's time for new ones. ❭ In hotter weather, keep cool with lighter-colored clothing. ❭ Wear a hat...

To prevent plantar fasciitis, wear good shoes with proper arch support. Stretch the Achilles tendon throughout the day, and flex your foot to stretch the tissue there.

Wear proper insoles and follow a routine of stretching, icing, and massaging. The tissue may be so tight that a massage will be very painful, but it will help relieve pain in the long run. You can also buy special boots that help stretch the tendon at night while you sleep.

ACHILLES TENDONITIS

Achilles tendonitis is when the Achilles tendon, which runs down the back of the leg, becomes swollen and painful due to overuse, arch problems, or insufficient stretching. In severe cases, the tendon can actually rupture, either partially or completely.

To prevent Achilles tendonitis, make sure you're stretching your calves and tendons. One way to do this is to place your foot on a wall and flex your toes upward.

As with many running injuries, icing your tendon can help alleviate the swelling and pain. Compression can help with swelling, and a shoe insert that lifts your heel can reduce the strain on the tendon.

ATHLETE'S FOOT

Athlete's foot is a fungal infection marked by itchy, scaly skin between your toes. You usually get it from moisture-filled areas like locker room showers and pools.

To prevent athlete's foot, wear clean socks and make sure your shoes are dry when you put them on. Try not to go barefoot in areas where you know multiple people are also not wearing shoes.

Drugstores sell many different creams and sprays that cure athlete's foot by killing the fungus. Don't tear off or scrape away the flaking skin—that just helps the fungus spread.

CHAFING

Chafing occurs when skin rubs against skin or against clothing, causing painful abrasions.

To prevent chafing, decrease the amount of friction on your skin. Apply Vaseline to the areas where you're experiencing the most chafing. Make sure that your clothes fit properly and that there aren't any loose hems or strings that might rub you the wrong way.

Chafing exposes new skin, so you'll need to treat the area. Wash it with water and dry it, then apply Neosporin or another topical antibiotic. Take some time off to allow your new skin to grow. Otherwise, it'll continue to rub and burn, and you might even get an infection.

INGROWN TOENAILS

An ingrown toenail is a toenail that has grown into the fleshy part of the toe around the nail, instead of growing outward like it's supposed to. You get these from poorly fitting shoes and poor foot care, and they can sideline you for weeks.

To prevent ingrown toenails, wear running shoes that fit you right and clip your toenails regularly. If your toenails are too long, they can hit the front of your shoe repeatedly, which can make them grow in the wrong direction. But don't clip them painfully short, either—that can cause ingrown toenails, too.

Sometimes over-the-counter products from companies like Dr. Scholl's work great. But sometimes the nail has to be lifted up and dug out of the surrounding skin, and it's best to let a professional handle it.

. . . or visor to keep the sun out of your eyes and limit sun damage on your face. 》 *Check discount stores for "last-season" deals to save some money*

42 RUNNING FOR WOMEN

IS THERE ANY RUNNING GEAR THAT YOU JUST CAN'T LIVE WITHOUT?

Michelle Gonzalez

1. GPS WATCH: My Garmin watch keeps me on track with my training. It gives me my splits, total distance, elevation for run, heart rate, and so much more—all with the touch of a button. These days, I also use it to keep me from going too fast (as I have a tendency to do on my easy-run days).

2. SPARKLY SOUL HEAD-BANDS: For years, I searched for a headband that would keep my hair and bangs out of my face and stay in place during long runs without giving me a headache. A couple of years ago I tried out Sparkly Soul headbands and have worn them on every single run since. These sparkly accessories are functional and fun at the same time.

3. TREADMILL: My husband and I purchased our treadmill almost four years ago, after our oldest son was born. Having a treadmill in our home allows me to run in the early morning hours without worrying about safety during the winter when the roads are covered in ice or snow and at night when my little boys are sleeping. It has given me an incredible amount of flexibility without my ever having to leave home.

4. ORANGE MUD VEST: Summer running is difficult and makes hydration even more important than it normally is. I've tried handheld bottles, belts, and CamelBaks but didn't have luck with any of them. The Orange Mud vest is the solution to this problem.

The idea behind it is that you use a bottle instead of a bladder-and-hose system. The bottle is kept behind you on your back, similar to a CamelBak or other bladder backpack systems. The bottle is easy to grab and replace thanks to a wide funnel opening and perfect retention.

when purchasing running gear. ❱ *If you like a certain model of shoe, find out when they'll be discontinued so you can stock up.*

4

RUNNING STRONG

"Believe that you can run farther or faster. Believe that you're young enough, old enough, strong enough, and so on to accomplish everything you want to do. Don't let worn-out beliefs stop you from moving beyond yourself."

JOHN BINGHAM, RUNNER, AUTHOR, AND SPEAKER

Every Part of You

Sometimes people think that the only thing you need to be a runner is strong legs. But in reality, running requires every part of your body—feet, legs, core, lungs, heart, and even arms—so it's important to stay in shape.

And don't forget the most important body part of all: your mind. When you run, you have to push yourself to new limits, and the only way to do that is to know your limits and understand how to push past them. A strong, positive outlook can keep you going even when you feel like quitting. Every time you go out for a training run, you're developing mental strength along with physical strength. If and when you sign up for a race, it's your mind that'll get you to the finish line when you don't think you can keep going.

In addition to mental fortitude, you'll also need a willing attitude and a big heart. Running can be hard, but it can also be an incredible journey that transforms your life. Pouring your heart into a run can even be a sort of emotional cleanse. It's just you, your body, and the pavement, working toward a goal you may have never thought possible, but which you'll soon achieve.

If it seems a little intimidating to get every single body part in shape, don't worry. Everyone has to start somewhere. As you incorporate running into your lifestyle over time, your body will get stronger, you'll be able to run faster and farther, and you'll feel healthier and happier.

BOSU BALLS

Core strength, leg strength, and balance are all important to running, and a BOSU ball can help you build all three. Regular old squats and lunges are great for this, too, but sometimes you want to change things up a little to keep your body from becoming too accustomed to your routine.

A BOSU ball has a flat, weighted base made of plastic and rubber, with an inflated rubber dome on top. Basically, it's a regular stability ball that's been cut in half. You can put either the stability-ball side up or the base side up and do different workout routines on both sides, including squats, lunges, and more. For example, you can put your feet on the base side and do push-ups, then switch to the stability-ball side and do sit-ups. Even just standing still on top of either side of the BOSU ball is a challenge, because it requires you to maintain your center of gravity on an unstable, constantly changing surface. That instability helps you develop muscles that are hard to workout otherwise. The BOSU ball is a versatile tool, and no matter how you use it, it will help you grow stronger and learn how to balance your body.

THOUGH YOUR ENTIRE BODY IS ENGAGED WHEN YOU GO FOR A RUN, THERE ARE SPECIFIC AREAS THAT ARE ESPECIALLY ESSENTIAL TO THIS

Be Good to Your Body

A healthy run begins with stretching. You want to keep your muscles loose and ready for the challenging activity ahead. If you get an injury two miles away from home because you didn't stretch out first, it's going to be a long, painful journey back. Stretching after your run is essential, too. Otherwise, lactic acid will build up in your muscles, making you feel sore and stiff. Here are some stretches to get you started.

WALKING LUNGE

The walking lunge stretches out your hamstrings and quads, both of which are pivotal to running. Start by taking a large step forward with your left leg. Bend at the knee until your thigh is parallel to the ground and your knee is in line with your ankle. Don't let your knee extend beyond your toe—this can cause serious injuries. Now push upward and bring both your legs together. Alternate your legs moving forward. Focus on keeping your knee behind your toe.

CALF STRETCH

Your calves can get extremely tight while running, especially when running on hilly terrain. You can do this calf stretch throughout the day, no matter where you are. Face a wall and put your hands against it at chest level. Press the ball of your left foot against the wall with your heel touching the ground. Keep your leg straight and lean toward the wall until you feel the stretch in your calf. You might also feel this stretch in the arch of your foot. Switch legs and repeat.

HAMSTRING STRETCH

Runners often have issues with their hamstrings, because these are some of the main muscles they use to propel themselves forward. If your hamstrings are too tight, you could end up with pulled muscles and back problems. To stretch them out, lie on your back and extend one leg. Try to keep your back flat, with your lower back touching the floor. Bend your left knee but keep your right leg extended straight out on the floor. Slowly straighten your right leg toward the ceiling and grab the back of your knee with both hands. Pull your leg toward your torso until you feel the stretch. Remember to be gentle; you can hurt yourself if you pull too hard or too fast. Switch legs and repeat.

ACTIVITY. HERE ARE THE 10 MAJOR MUSCLES ASSOCIATED WITH RUNNING: *QUADRICEPS are the four muscles on the front of your thighs that let . . .*

QUAD STRETCH

Your quads are the huge leg muscles in the front part of your upper thighs. It's good to stretch them while standing so that your hips stay aligned. To start, stand on one leg. Feel free to steady yourself against a wall or other object if you have trouble balancing. Bend one knee and bring it up behind you toward your glutes. Grab your ankle with one hand and hold the pose for 30 seconds to 1 minute. Switch legs and repeat.

IT BAND STRETCH

It's common for the IT band to get inflamed as you increase your mileage, so you definitely want to stretch it out before and after a run. While standing, cross your left leg in front of your right leg. Extend your right arm overhead and reach to the left. You should feel the stretch down the entire right side of your body. Switch sides and repeat.

SHOULDER STRETCH

They may not be doing as much hard work as your legs and feet, but your back and shoulders help keep your body upright and give you good form while running. Stretching them is just as important as stretching the rest of your body. Start by standing up straight and relaxing your shoulders. Put your left arm over your head, bending at the elbow so that your left hand is reaching behind your neck toward the center of your back. With your right arm, grip your left arm at the bent elbow and gently pull it toward your left ear. Try to get your hand as far down your back as you feel comfortable—but no farther! You don't want to strain or injure yourself.

FOAM ROLLING

Foam rolling is exactly what it sounds like: rolling a foam cylinder over your muscles and applying pressure. In the past, only professional athletes and physical therapists used this method, but now it's become common for anyone to do it.

What you're looking for when foam rolling is a "trigger point." Trigger points are knots that form at specific areas in your muscles because of overuse or insufficient stretching. Putting pressure on these trigger points is painful, but it's a great way to be proactive in your own injury prevention and recovery. It's comparable to deep-tissue massage, except that you get to control the amount of pressure and the place where it's applied. Foam rolling helps your muscles recover faster so you can get back to running and living pain-free.

Foam rolling can be uncomfortable, but it shouldn't be unbearable, so don't go too hard on yourself. You may feel a release of pressure as you continue to roll out the sore area.

Even if you're not experiencing any pain or tightness, foam rolling can help keep your muscles loose and injury-free. Do it proactively.

... you swing your legs forward and power up hills. 》 HAMSTRINGS MUSCLES, or "hammys," connect the upper back of your leg, helping you move forward

WHAT'S YOUR FAVORITE EXERCISE FOR RUNNING?

Elise Wallace

After running my first marathon, I vowed to never do it again. It was hard. It hurt. I hit that "wall" that everyone talks about. I thought I had done everything right to train, but looking back I can see I was inexperienced in my running world. I was a baby. There was so much information that I didn't know.

When I made the decision to attempt that distance again almost three years later, I was ready to change. I knew I could run a marathon, but now I was ready to get faster.

I already had the "long run" technique in my race plan, but what I needed was to incorporate speed into my training. How was I going to do this? With the help of the dreaded treadmill. Yes, some people call this machine a "dreadmill," but there's no reason to vilify this useful tool.

I will admit, the treadmill still gives me butterflies in my stomach every time I'm headed to a workout, but that's only because I know I'm about to do something hard. Get comfortable with being uncomfortable. Getting faster is not easy. . . that's why it feels so good to succeed at it.

My favorite treadmill workout is speed intervals, namely Yasso 800s. You can do them on a treadmill or a track. The theory behind this scary term is that your time in seconds and minutes for 10 rounds of 800 meters (½ mile) is your predicted marathon finish time in hours and minutes: Running your 800s in 4:30 will predict a 4 hour 30 minute marathon for you. But speed intervals aren't limited to marathon training. They can be incorporated into any race distance training. For a 5k, try one-minute intervals. Make sure you warm up, recover between each interval, and cool down at the end.

One of the reasons I love this workout so much is because you're able to see your speed increasing—it's quantifiable, you know it's working! Plus, you have a puddle of sweat on the ground to prove that you did something hard. Almost every single time I do speed intervals on the treadmill, I doubt my ability to finish, but that runner's high brings me back every time.

and bend your knees. ❭ *BICEPS are on the front of your upper arm and help maintain posture, keep your balance, and prevent your shoulders from tensing . . .*

RUNNING STRONG **49**

Runner's Workout

Running is the perfect exercise—almost. Even the best runners benefit from building their strength, flexibility, and endurance with other exercises. This workout will help you do all of that, and it takes less than 10 minutes. Try it twice a week and you'll feel yourself improving as a runner.

Start by loosening your neck, gently turning your head side-to-side. Straighten your arms in front of you and shake them out for 10 seconds. Do the same thing with your right leg and then the left leg.

Now you're going to do eight rounds of high-intensity and low-intensity exercises that will help strengthen your body and make you a better runner.

ROUTINE

WARM UP

2 MINUTES: Jumping Jacks (or Dancing)

ROUND 1

30 SECONDS: Sit Squats

30 SECONDS: Pilates Sit-ups

ROUND 2

30 SECONDS: High Knees

30 SECONDS: Forearm Plank

ROUND 3

30 SECONDS: Sit Squats

30 SECONDS: Pilates Sit-ups

ROUND 4

30 SECONDS: High Knees

30 SECONDS: Forearm Plank

WARM UP

JUMPING JACKS (OR DANCING)

1. Start with your feet together and hands at your sides. Engage your abdominal muscles by pretending you are bracing for a punch.

2. Jump both legs out to the side, landing with your feet spaced just wider than your hips while raising your arms overhead and clapping.

3. Bend your knees slightly while you jump again to bring your feet back together and your arms down to your side. Repeat.

Change It Up: Dance! Put on music you love and dance vigorously, moving arms and legs. You can also alternate sets of jumping jacks and dancing.

EXERCISES

SIT SQUATS

1. Start with your feet shoulder width apart and hands on your thighs.

2. Bend your knees and keep your back straight as if you're sitting in a chair and extend your arms in front of you.

. . . up while you run. 〉 NECK MUSCLES *let you hold your head up and keep your balance while running. Running can make them surprisingly sore, so try to*

50 RUNNING FOR WOMEN

(Alternatively, you can use a chair until you're familiar and comfortable with the exercise.)

3. With your arms extended in front of you, use your legs and abdominal muscles to press yourself back to a standing position. Repeat.

HIGH KNEES

Standing up, alternate lifting knees in quick succession as if marching. Keep your back straight (use good form).

PILATES SIT-UPS

1. Lie down on your back, bend your knees, and extend your arms along the ground at your sides.

2. Lift your shoulders, tighten your abdominal muscles, relax your neck (chin to chest), and pulse your arms up and down for 10 counts.

3. Return to the starting position. Repeat.

Change It Up: If you feel strain in your neck, do a regular crunch instead by bending your elbows, placing your fingertips behind your ears, and using your abdominal muscles to raise your shoulders up from the ground.

FOREARM PLANK

1. Extend your body lengthwise, stomach down, resting on your elbows and toes.

2. Keep your back flat and your hips a little elevated.

3. Hold this position for the length of the exercise.

4. Sit back on your heels to rest.

Change It Up: If planks are difficult at first, shorten the intervals to 10 seconds and build up to longer periods. Keep a watch with a second hand or a timer in front of your hands so you don't have to turn your neck to look at a clock.

stretch them out and keep them relaxed. ❭ *GLUTEAL MUSCLES in your buttocks bring your thighs in line with your body and help you move forward.*

Strength and Flexibility Workout

Want a more energetic, explosive stride when you're running? Try this workout once a week. It only takes a few minutes, and it'll have you kicking up dust on your next run.

Start by loosening your neck, gently turning your head side-to-side. Straighten your arms in front of you and shake them out for 10 seconds. Do the same thing with your right leg and then the left.

Now you are going to spend 60 seconds in each movement, and once the minute is up, move right into the next movement.

ROUTINE

WARM UP
2 MINUTES: Jumping Jacks and/or Dancing

ROUND 1
60 SECONDS: Forearm Plank

ROUND 2
30 SECONDS: Side Plank, right

30 SECONDS: Side Plank, left

ROUND 3
60 SECONDS: Superman

ROUND 4
60 SECONDS: Hollow Rock

MINUTE 5
60 SECONDS: Lunges

REPEAT ROUNDS 1 THROUGH 4 ONCE

WARM UP

JUMPING JACKS AND/OR DANCING

You can always choose to put on your favorite song and dance around for a couple of minutes.

EXERCISES

FOREARM PLANK

SIDE PLANK (RIGHT SIDE AND LEFT SIDE)

Change it up: If you're new to planks, you can modify the side plank by bending your top leg and placing it in front of you, foot flat on the matt and knee up.

ACHILLES TENDONS *are the thickest tendons in your body, which enable you to bend and flex your ankles.* ❭ *The HEART works extra hard when you're running.* ❭

SUPERMAN

Lie on your stomach with straight arms overhead, next to your ears. At the same time, lift your arms and legs, hold, and relax. Repeat multiple times for 1 minute.

LUNGES (LEFT SIDE AND RIGHT SIDE)

1. Start by standing with your feet a bit wider than shoulder width apart.

2. Take a big step forward with your left foot. Make sure your knees, hips, and shoulders are all facing forward.

3. Sink straight down until your left knee is at a 90-degree angle and you are on your back toes. Make sure that your left knee is directly above your ankle.

4. Push back into the starting position. Switch sides.

HOLLOW ROCK

1. Lie flat, arms overhead.

2. At the same time, lift up your straight arms and straight legs into a "V."

3. Hold for the length of the exercise.

Change it up: If holding this posture for 1 minute is too challenging, hold the "V" as long as you can. Return to the starting position and repeat the exercise as many times as you need to in 1 minute.

ABDOMINAL MUSCLES line the abdominal wall along your stomach. These help keep your posture upright and alleviate back pain when you're running.

ody Blaster Workout

Are you ready for this? If you're running to slim down and strengthen up, then this workout is the cherry on top of everything you've accomplished so far. At first you'll feel a burn. But before long you'll be eating the burn for breakfast. Try this once a week.

Start by loosening your neck, gently turning your head side-to-side. Straighten your arms in front of you and shake them out for 10 seconds. Do the same thing with your right leg and then the left.

Now you'll do 8 rounds of 40 seconds of high-intensity work followed by 20 seconds of low-intensity work.

ROUTINE

WARM UP
2 MINUTES: Jumping Jacks and/or Dancing

ROUND 1
40 SECONDS: Mountain Climbers

20 SECONDS: Mountain Climbers (slow and controlled)

ROUND 2
40 SECONDS: Burpees

20 SECONDS: Mountain Climbers (slow and controlled)

ROUND 3
40 SECONDS: Push-Ups

20 SECONDS: Mountain Climbers (slow and controlled)

CONTINUE ALTERNATING ROUNDS UNTIL YOU HAVE COMPLETED A TOTAL OF 3 ROUNDS.

WARM UP

JUMPING JACKS AND/OR DANCING

Put on your favorite playlist and dance!

EXERCISES

MOUNTAIN CLIMBERS (RIGHT SIDE AND LEFT SIDE)

1. Start on the floor in a push-up or plank position—arms straight beneath your shoulders and legs together and straight behind you.

2. Squeeze your glutes, tighten your abs, keep your back straight, and look between your hands.

3. Shift your lower-body weight to the right leg and bend your left knee toward your left hand. If you were standing upright, you would look like you are climbing a mountain.

4. Now repeat the movement with your right leg.

CALF MUSCLES are located on the lower back of your legs. They help move you forward and stabilize you while running. ❯ *IT BANDS are located along the*

BURPEES

1. Start by squatting down. With straight arms, place your hands directly under your shoulders, just outside of shoulder width, as you would for a push-up.

2. Walk or jump your feet back into a plank position. Plant your toes into the floor, squeeze your glutes, and brace your abs. Your body should form a straight line from your head to your ankles.

3. Lower yourself to the bottom for a push-up. (You can also drop to your knees here if the push-ups feel too difficult).

4. Tighten your glutes and abs, and push up to return to plank position—either from your knees or from your toes.

5. Jump your feet back in toward your hands, and jump up to standing. Repeat.

PUSH-UPS

1. Start in a plank position, with straight arms beneath your shoulders, back straight, and level head with eyes looking between your hands.

2. Slowly lower your body, and then press up to straight arms.

3. Keep your hips level; don't let them drop down. Push-ups are all about form!

outside of your thighs and run the entire length of your legs. Their main job is to extend your legs and help your hips rotate.

5
FUEL UP!

"Ask yourself: 'Can I give more?'
The answer is usually: 'Yes.'"

PAUL TERGAT, KENYAN
PROFESSIONAL MARATHONER

Burning Calories

One of the best parts about running? Eating! When you run, you're burning a ton of calories, so you can enjoy a few extra treats every now and then. Food is what fuels you, both in your daily life and when you run. Make smart decisions about food and you will become a better runner with a happier, healthier lifestyle.

Keeping track of what you're eating and how your body feels when you're running is really important. If you feel a little lackluster on a morning run, it might be because of what you ate the night before. A tough evening run can be even tougher with a bulky lunch lingering in your stomach. Paying attention to your eating habits can help you get the most out of your meals and make sure that what you're eating is helping, not hindering, your body.

Normally, I have a stomach of steel, so when I started getting sick while running, I didn't understand what I was doing wrong. I didn't want to be barfing on the side of the road or spending precious minutes in a Porta Potty during a race. It was really frustrating! But I took a closer look at my diet, and after a bit of trial and error, I figured out what to eat and what not to eat to keep myself in peak condition. I encourage you to do the same, whether you're getting sick on the trail or just want to stay healthy—running is all about what works for you.

LOSING WEIGHT

Many people turn to running to lose weight. It's a great way to raise your heart rate, get in your recommended daily cardio, and keep yourself at your happy weight. If you track your runs with an app, you can use it to see how many calories you're burning. If one of your running goals is to lose weight, you need to burn more calories than you consume daily. This may sound like a simple equation, but it's actually a careful balance. You don't want to indulge in too many calories, but at the same time, you need to make sure that your body has enough fuel.

When you first start running, you may feel extra hungry. Don't go overboard, but make sure you're not starving yourself, either. A food journal can be a helpful way to keep track of where you're getting your calories every day.

If you do want to lose weight by running, consistency is key. Try to run three to four days a week to keep your metabolism going at a steady rate. If you're only running one to two days a week, it will take longer to see results—but it may be a good starting point if you haven't been exercising much lately and need to ease into a more active lifestyle.

Eat for Your Run

What you eat makes a big difference in the way you run. Eating too much processed junk food can make you feel sluggish and bloated, while eating healthy food can make you feel better and run faster. Below are some tips about the kinds of food that will let you perform your best while running. If you're making big changes to your diet, remember to make them gradually and see how your body reacts. Change is good, but too much change at once can end up hurting you in the long run.

PROTEIN

Proteins are long chains of amino acids that play many essential roles in the human body, including building muscles. Foods high in protein include meat, poultry, seafood, eggs, tofu and other soy products, beans, peas, nuts, and seeds. You can also buy protein powder, usually made from soy or whey, which you can add to baked goods, smoothies, and more.

Because protein helps build muscles, adding more of it to your diet will make your muscles get stronger and recover more quickly. Also, when you increase your activity, you'll find yourself hungry more often, and protein will help you feel full for longer than carbohydrates. The Institute of Medicine recommends that 10 to 35 percent of your daily calories come from protein. For adult women, that's usually about 46 grams a day, but if you start eating more as a runner, then that number might be higher.

FAT

Don't be scared of fat—having some in your diet is important. Fats provide your body with energy, store nutrients, and help regulate your body temperature. Instead of avoiding them, go for healthy fats, like monounsaturated fats, polyunsaturated fats, and omega-3 fatty acids. These healthy fats play a role in energy storage, brain development, blood clotting, and inflammation management. You can find them in foods like fish, olive oil, canola oil, avocados, olives, nuts, and peanut butter. I love adding peanut butter to my smoothie after a workout, because it gives me a great energy boost right when I'm feeling depleted. In the "2010 Dietary Guidelines for Americans," the USDA recommends that adults get 20 to 35 percent of their daily calories from fat.

CARBOHYDRATES

Carbs are a huge part of a runner's diet. Your body relies on them for energy, which you need a lot of when you're training for or running a race. But it's important to get the right kind of carbs at the right times for maximum performance. Consuming carbs right before, during, and right after a run can help provide you with long-lasting energy. Ever heard of "carb loading"? There's a reason people eat huge amounts of carbs the night before a long run—it gives you the sustained energy you need the next morning.

According to a 2010 article in *Today's Dietician*, runners should get at least 55 percent of their daily calories from carbohydrates while training and 55 to 60 percent before a race or long-training run. Add bananas, brown rice, oatmeal, whole-grain bread, pasta, and—a runner's favorite—beer, to your diet for some delicious carbs that'll keep you going on your next run.

SUGAR

Sugar is one specific kind of carbohydrate. Like any carbohydrate, it can give you energy, but your body converts sugar into fat much more easily than it does most other carbohydrates. And because of the way your body processes sugar, the burst of energy it gives you can be quickly followed by a crash, whereas lower-sugar foods can carry you farther into the run. It's important to be aware of how much sugar is in your energy bars and sports drinks. Even though they claim to be "healthy" and great for "athletes," many are packed with sugar and other unhealthy additives.

Fruit is a healthy source of sugar, since the natural sugars they contain are offset by fiber, vitamins, and minerals. But sugary foods, such as cookies, cake, and anything with high-fructose corn syrup should be enjoyed only in small quantities. They're fun to eat once in a while, but they won't help your running performance.

ELECTROLYTES

Electrolytes are molecules that help keep you properly hydrated and play an essential role in your muscular and nervous systems. One common electrolyte is table salt. Not every runner needs to increase their electrolyte intake when they first start, but if you sweat heavily or run in hot temperatures, you should definitely look into it, because you lose electrolytes when you sweat. If your electrolyte levels get too low, you might experience dehydration and muscle cramping, both of which can be huge issues.

Electrolytes exist in natural sources like milk, coconut water, bananas, and raisins, but many runners rely on sports drinks like Gatorade. The only problem? Sports drinks tend to be high in sugar. To avoid that sugar, try consuming more natural sources of electrolytes or one of the many new products that serve as an alternative to Gatorade. You can even make your own sports drink at home, or take salt tablets on your run with you.

WATER

Water plays many vital roles in the human body, like bringing nutrients and oxygen to your cells and carrying wastes and toxins away. Water is key for runners, as dehydration can be crippling. And once you start experiencing dehydration symptoms, drinking too much water too quickly can be harmful—even fatal, in some circumstances—so it's really important to stay hydrated at all times.

The average person should be drinking 2 to 2.5 liters daily, and about one-third of that is met by food intake. If you feel thirsty while you run, bring some water with you and take a few swigs when you're stopped at a stoplight or just need to feel refreshed.

5 SUPER FOODS

CHIA SEEDS are a natural superfood, chock-full of protein, fiber, and omega-3 fatty acids. They even help you stay hydrated.

SALMON is an excellent source of omega-3 fatty acids, which help your heart and muscles when you exercise a lot.

CHERRIES are one of the most antioxidant-rich fruits on earth and help with muscle recovery and soreness.

CHOCOLATE MILK is a great recovery option, rich in carbohydrates, proteins, and electrolytes.

PEANUT BUTTER is full of healthy fat and protein and gives you a sustained release of energy that's perfect for a workout.

EATING ON THE RUN— LITERALLY!

When you start running longer distances, it's important to replenish your body's fuel supplies not just before and after you run, but also while you're out running. Your body can only sustain you for so long— that's why many long-distance runners have to bring something to eat along with them. If you start to feel sluggish and tired when running for 60 minutes or more, it may be time to start packing a snack.

Many runners opt for energy gels or energy chews, which can be easy to get down when running. But not everyone finds these products tasty or easily digestible (I'm not a fan, personally), so you may want to try a different option, like sport jelly beans, pretzels, or anything else with a lot of carbohydrates and electrolytes.

Start experimenting with different foods and gels, and see what works for you. Whatever you choose, stash it in your shorts pockets or running belt during your next run. About halfway into the run, slow down and have a quick snack. Chew extra thoroughly so you don't choke, and wash it down with some water. You'll notice a big difference in your energy levels as soon as the food gets into your system.

For an 18-mile run, I eat at miles 6, 12, and 16 and drink water every 2 to 3 miles, depending on the weather. You may need to eat and drink more or less than that. Whatever your body is comfortable with is what's right for you.

Runner Recipes

It's important to increase your calories the night before a longer run to make sure that you have fuel for the following day. Again, it may take some trial and error to find what works for you and your body. You may find that the traditional pasta load the night before a run is too much for you, or you may find it's just the thing you need. Just be aware of how you're feeling and how your stomach is doing the following morning when running. Don't switch things up before a race—it's not a good time to encounter unexpected digestive problems.

The night before a race, I usually have pizza and a beer for dinner, since both of these foods are great sources of carbs. Some people swear by heavy carbs like pasta, but I've learned that my stomach doesn't process them well, and they make me feel heavy and bloated the next day.

The morning of the run, I stick to light foods, like bland oatmeal or toast topped with just a swipe of peanut butter. After I'm done running, I make sure to load up on protein-rich foods like a smoothie with protein powder or even a nice big cheeseburger, depending on how far I ran.

The following recipes include a great balance of nutrients to help you succeed while running. I've included three pre-run recipes, two recipes to gear up for a big run, three post-run recipes to help replenish your body, and three treat recipes. Remember, when you're running, it's super important to eat more than normal because you're burning a lot of calories and you need the fuel. One of the best parts of running is being able to eat a few extra treats every now and then.

CUT THESE OUT

SODA isn't just packed with sugar and empty calories—it can also dehydrate you.

DAIRY before a run is usually a bad idea because it can upset your stomach and make you feel bloated.

HIGH-FIBER FOODS should be avoided right before a run because they get the digestive tract moving, and that's the last thing you want to deal with while running. Caffeine can also cause the runs on a run.

FROZEN MEALS can be an easy option for dinner, but they're usually packed with sodium, which can interrupt your normal fluid balance and throw off your running.

SPORTS DRINKS are easy to grab on the go, but check the ingredients list—if there's a lot of sugar, the cost may outweigh the benefits.

WHOLE-GRAIN SWEET POTATO AND BUTTERMILK MUFFINS

MAKES 12 MUFFINS

Buttermilk makes these muffins light and fluffy and mashed sweet potato keeps them super moist. You can use leftover baked sweet potatoes or cook one in the microwave for 6 to 8 minutes until tender. You can even substitute canned pureed pumpkin if you like.

2½ cups whole-wheat flour

¾ cup sugar

2 teaspoons baking powder

1 teaspoon ground ginger

¼ teaspoon baking soda

¼ teaspoon salt

¼ cup melted unsalted butter

¼ cup vegetable oil

1 cup pureed or mashed cooked sweet potato

1 egg, beaten

½ cup buttermilk

1. Preheat the oven to 375°F.

2. Spray a 12-cup muffin tin with nonstick cooking spray or line with paper liners.

3. In a large bowl, stir together the flour, sugar, baking powder, ginger, baking soda, and salt.

4. In a medium bowl, combine the butter, oil, sweet potato, egg, and buttermilk and whisk until well combined. Add the wet mixture to the dry mixture, stirring gently just until combined.

5. Scoop the batter into the prepared muffin tin, filling each well about three-quarters full. Bake for 20 to 25 minutes, until a toothpick inserted into the center comes out clean. Transfer to a wire rack to cool. Serve warm or at room temperature.

BANANA-CINNAMON OATMEAL WITH WALNUTS

SERVES 1

Oatmeal is a popular breakfast for runners on race day because it is filling, provides plenty of carbs, and is easy to digest. This version is spiced up with a dash of cinnamon, sweetened with a bit of honey and bananas, and gets a nice crunch from chopped walnuts.

1⅓ cups water

⅔ cup rolled oats

2 teaspoons honey

¼ teaspoon cinnamon

⅛ teaspoon salt

½ medium banana, diced

½ cup low-fat milk or nondairy milk substitute (almond, rice, hemp, or soy)

1 tablespoon chopped walnuts, for garnish

1. In a medium saucepan, bring the water to a boil. Stir in the oats, honey, cinnamon, and salt. Reduce the heat to low and cook, uncovered and stirring occasionally, for about 5 minutes, until the oats are tender and the water has been mostly absorbed.

2. Stir in the banana and milk and return to a simmer. Cook for about 5 more minutes, stirring occasionally, until the mixture is thick. Remove from the heat, cover, and let sit for about 5 minutes before serving. Serve hot, garnished with the walnuts.

BLUEBERRY-OATMEAL BREAKFAST BARS

MAKES 8 BARS

These lightly sweetened fruit and oat bars are a perfect make-ahead breakfast. Wrap them individually and store them in the refrigerator or freezer for those mornings when you need something you can grab on the run.

FOR THE BARS

¼ cup coconut oil

3 tablespoons honey or maple syrup

3 tablespoons nut butter (peanut, almond, cashew, etc.)

2½ cups rolled oats

1 cup blueberries

FOR THE YOGURT TOPPING

1 tablespoon plain yogurt

1 tablespoon orange juice

1. Preheat the oven 350°F.

2. Line a 10-by-10-inch baking dish with parchment paper.

3. In a medium saucepan, combine the coconut oil, honey, and nut butter and heat for about 3 minutes over medium heat, stirring occasionally, until melted. Stir in the oats and then gently fold in the blueberries.

4. Transfer the mixture into the prepared baking dish and spread out. Bake until the sides just begin to turn brown, about 20 minutes.

5. Remove from the oven and let cool for 10 minutes. Using the parchment to lift the oat mixture from the pan, transfer it to a wire rack to cool completely. You can cool the bars either at room temperature or in the refrigerator.

6. Once cooled completely, make the yogurt topping. In a small bowl, combine the yogurt with the orange juice and drizzle the mixture over the oatmeal bars in diagonal lines. Cut into 8 rectangular bars. Store in the refrigerator for up to 3 days or in the freezer for up to 3 months. Bring to room temperature before serving.

WHOLE-WHEAT SPAGHETTI WITH FAST BOLOGNESE SAUCE

SERVES 4

Whole-wheat pasta is a great high-carb choice for the night before a big run. Here it's topped with a meaty Bolognese sauce that tastes like it has been simmered for hours but only takes about 30 minutes to cook.

8 ounces whole-wheat spaghetti

1 tablespoon extra-virgin olive oil

1 medium onion, finely chopped

2 medium carrots, finely chopped

2 medium stalks celery, finely chopped

3 garlic cloves, minced

8 ounces lean (93% or leaner) ground beef

⅓ cup dry red wine

1 (14-ounce) can petite-diced tomatoes

2 tablespoons tomato paste

⅛ teaspoon ground nutmeg

¼ teaspoon salt

¼ teaspoon freshly ground pepper

1. Bring a large pot of salted water to a boil. Add the pasta and cook according to the package directions. Drain.

2. Meanwhile, in a large, nonstick skillet over medium heat, heat the oil. Add the onion, carrots, celery, and garlic, and cook, stirring occasionally, for about 8 minutes until the vegetables are softened.

3. Add the meat to the skillet and cook, breaking up the meat with a spatula or wooden spoon, until browned, 3 to 4 minutes.

4. Raise the heat to medium–high, stir in the wine, and cook until most of the liquid has evaporated, about 2 minutes. Stir in the tomatoes, tomato paste, and nutmeg. Lower the heat to medium–low, cover, and simmer for 15 minutes. Add the salt and pepper and serve hot, spooned over the cooked pasta.

FIRED UP PIZZA WITH TURKEY SAUSAGE AND CARAMELIZED FENNEL

SERVES 4

A high-carb meal like pizza will fuel you through your run the next morning. This one is full of flavor from caramelized fennel and healthy turkey sausage.

- 1 tablespoon extra-virgin olive oil
- 1 fennel bulb, cored and cut into very thin slices
- 1 teaspoon sugar
- ¼ teaspoon salt
- 2 links Italian turkey sausage, casing removed
- 1 pound prepared pizza dough (ideally made with whole-wheat flour, at room temperature)
- 1 cup prepared tomato sauce or pizza sauce
- 1 cup shredded fontina cheese or part-skim mozzarella cheese

1. Preheat the oven to 500°F.

2. In a large skillet over medium-high heat, heat the oil. Add the fennel and cook, stirring frequently, for about 5 minutes, until the fennel is softened. Stir in the sugar and salt and cook, stirring occasionally, until the fennel is golden brown, about 15 to 20 minutes more. Transfer the fennel to a plate.

3. In the same pan, cook the sausage over medium-high heat, breaking it up with a wooden spoon, until cooked through, about 4 minutes. Drain off any excess oil.

4. Turn the dough out onto a lightly floured work surface and press or roll it out into a rough rectangle. Place the dough on a large, rimmed baking sheet (the dough rectangle should be about the size of the pan) and spoon the sauce over it, spreading it evenly with the back of the spoon.

5. Scatter the cheese over the sauce and top with the sausage and fennel, distributing them evenly over the pizza. Bake until the crust is crisp and lightly browned and the cheese is melted and bubbly, 15 to 20 minutes. Serve immediately.

WHAT'S YOUR FAVORITE FOOD TO EAT BEFORE A BIG RUN?

Nina Moore

Several years ago, I lost a significant amount of weight. By altering my daily diet and adding running to my routine, I not only changed the way I looked, but also gained a new confidence that I didn't even know was lacking in my life. The change in my energy was incredible, and I haven't turned back since.

Food is life, and I savor every bite. Good, healthy food can taste incredible and make you feel great. I try to stick to the 85:15 rule. Lean protein, fruit, and vegetables make up 85 percent of my daily intake. I eat very few items that come in a package, and healthy eating is a passion of mine.

Because I'm a human, I like to save 15 percent to have fun with. I'm Italian. I love pasta and wine. I make an incredible homemade pizza dough on Friday nights, and I could never live this life without ice cream. I believe in a realistic balance.

Fueling up for a run is unique to every individual. What works for me might not work for everyone, and that is okay. So much of what is written about what to eat before running focuses on "carb loading," but I have found over the years that it just doesn't work for me. I ran my first half marathon in the fall of 2014 and learned a lot about my body and how

I can best fuel for longer distances. When I set out for big runs while I trained, almond butter was my go-to. I often sliced half of an apple and dipped the slices in 1 to 2 tablespoons of almond butter. It's not too heavy on my stomach and never makes me feel gross while running. The combo of the protein and the natural sugars in the apple gives me the perfect amount of energy to get my miles in.

SUPER BERRY PROTEIN SMOOTHIE

SERVES 1

After a big run, your main goals are to rehydrate and fill up on protein to help your muscles repair themselves. This delicious smoothie helps you do both.

¾ cup water
1 cup spinach
2 cups frozen mixed berries
½ cup plain, low-fat or nondairy yogurt
2 scoops vanilla protein powder
1 tablespoon walnuts
1 tablespoon ground flaxseed

Place all of the ingredients in a blender and process until smooth. Serve immediately.

FLUFFY QUINOA AND APPLE PANCAKES

SERVES 4

These healthy pancakes are made with whole-wheat flour and protein-packed quinoa. They make a great post-run recovery breakfast or brunch.

2 cups cooked and cooled quinoa

1½ cups whole-wheat flour

4 teaspoons baking powder

1 teaspoon coarse salt

2 teaspoons cinnamon

1 teaspoon freshly ground nutmeg

¼ ground flaxseed

2 eggs, plus 2 egg whites

2 tablespoons neutral-flavored oil such as grape seed, safflower, or sunflower seed, plus more for preparing the skillet, divided

¾ cup nonfat milk

¼ cup maple syrup, plus more for serving, divided

2 apples, diced small

1. In a medium bowl, stir together the quinoa, flour, baking powder, salt, cinnamon, nutmeg, and flaxseed.

2. In a separate medium bowl, place the eggs, egg whites, oil, milk, and maple syrup and whisk to combine. Whisk the egg mixture into the quinoa mixture and then gently fold in the diced apples.

3. Use oil to lightly coat a nonstick skillet and heat over medium heat. Spoon the batter into the skillet, using about ¼ cup per pancake and gently flattening with the back of the spoon. Cook until bubbles form on the top and the bottom is golden brown, about 2 to 3 minutes, and then turn over and cook for 2 to 3 minutes more until the second side is golden brown. Serve hot with a drizzle of maple syrup.

GRILLED SKIRT STEAK TACOS WITH AVOCADO SALSA

SERVES 4

Steak is the perfect thing for satisfying a post-run appetite. Here it's rubbed with chile powder and other spices, grilled, and then tucked into warm corn tortillas and topped with a rich and refreshing avocado salsa.

FOR THE TACOS

1 tablespoon chili powder

2 garlic cloves, minced

¼ teaspoon cinnamon

¼ teaspoon salt

Pinch cayenne

1¼ pound skirt steak, about 1-inch thick

12 corn tortillas

3 cups shredded red cabbage

½ cup chopped cilantro

1 lime, cut into wedges

FOR THE SALSA

1 large cucumber, peeled, seeded, and diced

2 avocados, diced

½ red onion, diced

Juice of 2 limes

2 jalapeno chiles, chopped (remove and discard the seeds for a milder salsa)

¼ cup chopped cilantro

Salt

TO PREPARE THE STEAK:

1. In a small bowl, stir together the chili powder, garlic, cinnamon, salt, and cayenne. Rub the mixture into the steak on both sides.

2. Preheat a grill or a grill pan to medium-high heat. Grill the steaks, flipping them over once, until seared on the outside and cooked to desired doneness, about 5 to 6 minutes per side for medium rare. Transfer the steak to a platter and let them rest for about 10 minutes.

TO MAKE THE SALSA:

In a large bowl, toss together the cucumber, avocados, and onion. Add the lime juice, chiles, and cilantro, and season with salt. Toss to combine.

TO ASSEMBLE THE TACOS:

Heat each tortilla on the grill for about 30 seconds per side. Fill with some of the sliced steak, a handful of shredded cabbage, and a dollop of the salsa. Sprinkle with the cilantro and serve with a lime wedge.

CHOCOLATE CHUNK ALMOND COOKIES

MAKES ABOUT 10 COOKIES

These grain-free almond cookies are loaded with chocolate. They are also full of the protein you need to recover.

½ cup unflavored or vanilla protein powder

¼ cup almond butter, plus 2 tablespoons

¼ cup coconut palm sugar

2 teaspoons coconut oil

½ cup almond milk (or substitute another nondairy alternative)

½ cup ground almonds

2 ounces dark chocolate, chopped

1. Preheat the oven to 350°F.

2. Line a baking sheet with parchment paper.

3. In a medium bowl, combine the protein powder, almond butter, sugar, coconut oil, almond milk, and ground almonds, and mix well. Stir in the chocolate chunks.

4. Roll the cookie dough into 1½-inch balls and place them on the prepared baking sheet lined with parchment paper. Flatten each ball with the back of a fork.

5. Bake for 10 to 12 minutes. Let cool to room temperature on the baking sheet. Serve at room temperature or store in an airtight container.

WHOLE-WHEAT GINGER SNACK CAKE

SERVES 8

This satisfying spice cake is sweetened with a combination of brown sugar, maple syrup, and blackstrap molasses, a surprisingly healthy sweetener that's loaded with calcium, iron, copper, manganese, magnesium, and potassium. Carrot juice is a secret ingredient that adds both moistness and beta-carotene.

⅔ cup milk or nondairy milk substitute (rice, soy, hemp, or almond)

⅓ cup carrot juice

¼ cup molasses

¼ cup maple syrup

1 tablespoon apple cider vinegar

2 tablespoons melted coconut oil

2 tablespoons ground flaxseed

1 cup whole-wheat flour

¼ cup brown sugar

1½ teaspoons ground ginger

1½ teaspoons cinnamon

1 teaspoon baking soda

½ teaspoon allspice

¼ teaspoon salt

1. Preheat the oven to 400°F.
2. Coat an 8-by-8-inch baking pan lightly with nonstick cooking spray or coconut oil.
3. In a medium bowl, whisk together the milk, carrot juice, molasses, maple syrup, vinegar, coconut oil, and flaxseed. Set aside to rest for 5 to 10 minutes.
4. In a large bowl, combine the flour, sugar, ginger, cinnamon, baking soda, allspice, and salt.
5. Pour the wet ingredients into the flour mixture and stir just to combine. Pour the batter into the prepared baking pan and bake for 25 minutes. Remove from the oven and let rest for 20 minutes before serving.

CHOCOLATE CAKE

SERVES 12

*There is nothing healthy about this choco-
late cake recipe. But if you've been running,
sticking to your routine, and going farther and
faster than ever before, then you deserve an
indulgence now and then. Enjoy!*

FOR THE CAKE

1 cup (2 sticks) unsalted butter, cut into
chunks, plus additional for greasing

1½ cups all-purpose flour, plus additional
for dusting

4 (1-ounce) squares bittersweet chocolate,
finely chopped

¾ cup high-quality cocoa powder

1 tablespoon baking powder

1 teaspoon baking soda

½ teaspoon salt

4 large eggs, beaten

1½ cups granulated sugar

2 teaspoons pure vanilla extract

1 cup sour cream, divided

1 cup mini dark chocolate chips

FOR THE FROSTING

1 cup (2 sticks) salted butter

¾ cup high-quality cocoa powder

4 ounces high-quality semi-sweet
chocolate, melted and cooled

1 teaspoon instant coffee

3 to 3½ cups confectioners' sugar

2 tablespoons heavy cream

TO MAKE THE CAKE:

1. Preheat the oven to 350°F.

2. Grease and flour 2 (8-inch) round cake
pans and set aside.

3. Place a medium saucepan with 2 inches
of water over medium heat. Set a metal
bowl over it, being careful the bowl does
not touch the water. Bring the water to a
simmer. Reduce the heat to maintain the
temperature.

4. Add the unsalted butter and chopped
bittersweet chocolate to the bowl. Stir for
2 to 3 minutes, or until melted
and smooth.

5. Remove the bowl from the heat. Set aside
for about 15 minutes, or until the chocolate mixture cools to room temperature.

6. In a medium bowl, sift together the flour,
cocoa powder, baking powder, baking
soda, and salt.

7. In a large bowl, using a whisk or hand
mixer, beat the eggs, sugar, and vanilla
for about 1 minute, or until thoroughly
mixed.

8. Add the cooled chocolate-butter mixture
to the egg mixture, and beat for 1 minute more, or until all ingredients are
incorporated.

9. Add the flour mixture to the chocolate
mixture, alternating with the sour cream,
in 3 batches, starting and ending with the
flour. Mix well after each addition. ❯

10. Fold the chocolate chips into the batter until evenly distributed.

11. Spoon the batter into the prepared cake pans and smooth the tops.

12. Put the cake pans on the middle rack of the preheated oven, and bake for 30 to 35 minutes, or until a toothpick inserted into the center comes out clean and the cake tops spring back when lightly touched.

13. Remove the cakes from the oven, and cool for 10 minutes.

14. Run a knife along the edge of the cakes, and carefully pop them out of the pans. Cool completely on wire racks before frosting.

TO MAKE THE FROSTING:

1. In a large bowl, using a hand mixer, beat the butter for about 3 minutes, or until fluffy and pale.

2. Add the cocoa powder and beat for about 1 minute, or until smooth.

3. Stir in the melted, cooled chocolate and coffee. Beat for 1 minute to combine.

4. Add the confectioners' sugar, 1 cup at a time, beating to incorporate after each addition and scraping down the sides of the bowl as needed.

5. When you achieve the desired sweetness, adjust the thickness of the frosting with the heavy cream as needed.

TO ASSEMBLE THE FINISHED CAKE:

1. Place 1 cooled cake layer on a cake board or serving plate.

2. Thickly spread about one-third of the frosting over the layer right to the edge.

3. Top with the second cooled cake layer, pressing down firmly.

4. Generously frost the sides of the cake with another one-third of the frosting and the top with the remaining one-third of the frosting.

5. Cover and refrigerate the cake until ready to serve.

6. Allow the cake to sit at room temperature for 2 hours to soften the frosting before slicing it into generous pieces.

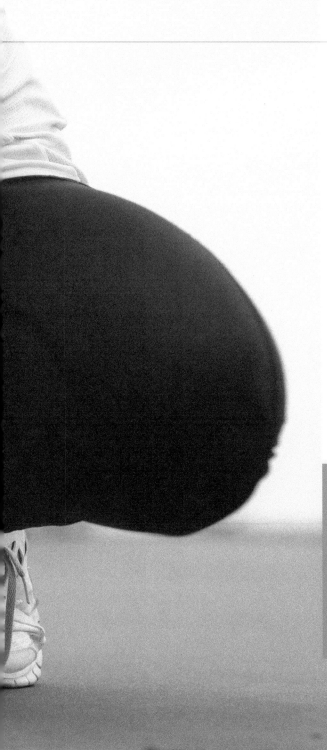

6
HIT THE
ROAD

"I often hear someone say I'm not a real runner. We are all runners, some just run faster than others. I never met a fake runner."

BART YASSO, RUNNER AND "CHIEF RUNNING OFFICER" AT *RUNNER'S WORLD*

Train Your Body

When you're first beginning to run, you want to focus on getting comfortable and enjoying the run. But soon you'll probably start itching for something more—and training plans can help you get there. They can be intimidating, but just remember that these plans are meant to help you succeed and make the most of your running, not to make you feel guilty or stressed out. A training plan can help keep you consistent, and with consistency comes improvement. Even if you're not training for a specific race, following a plan can help you reach your health goals and stay motivated. If you keep a running journal or track your runs with an app, you'll get the thrill of watching your performance gradually improve over time.

When looking for the right training plan, there are a few things to keep in mind: your time commitment, your current level of fitness, and how much time you need to reach your goal. Make sure you pick feasible goals and give yourself enough time to train for them. It's great to work toward a huge milestone, but make sure you set smaller goals along the way, so you don't get burned out and quit or overwork yourself and get injured. If you've never run before, starting out with a 14-week marathon plan may be a bit over-zealous, but an 8-week 5K run/walk program might be perfect.

> **The difference between a jogger and a runner is an entry blank.**
>
> GEORGE SHEEHAN, RUNNING WRITER

There's a plan out there for everyone. What's most important is finding one that fits your lifestyle. If all you want to do is run a mile in under 15 minutes, that's great. Be proud of yourself for taking the initiative, committing to a training plan, and setting feasible goals. You can work toward bigger goals in the future, if and when you're ready.

10 TIPS FOR VARYING YOUR TRAINING RUNS: *Try a new route that includes hills to work on your quad strength. Run on a new surface. If you normally stick*

Farther and Faster

If you want to run faster and farther, increase the length and speed of your runs in small increments.

Let's say you want to up your mileage. Once or twice a week, designate a "long run" day where you'll run farther than usual. That could mean 2 miles, 20 miles, or anything in between. Whatever distance you choose is the "base" of your long run. Every week, add half a mile to that base. So if you're starting at 2 miles, bring it up to 2.5 the next week, and then 3 the week after that. After a lot of training, you can even start adding full miles from week to week. The long run is where your endurance training really counts, and increasing your mileage slowly means you're less likely to get injured, burned out, or scared off.

If you want to increase your speed, you'll love intervals—short bursts of faster running during your normal run. If you're just starting out and you force yourself to run 3 miles as fast as you possibly can, you'll be so sore the next day that you'll never want to run again. With intervals, you push yourself to run faster, but only for short, sustainable periods of time.

Start out with a warm up of 5 to 10 minutes or 1 to 2 miles, whatever you're comfortable with. Warming up and cooling down are especially important for speed workouts, because you're using different muscles than normal and you don't want any injuries or extra soreness. After the warm up, run the next mile or miles at a faster pace. Then return to your regular speed.

Here's an example of an awesome track workout that you can do to increase your speed.

) Start with a three-lap warm up.

) Stretch.

) Run one lap at a faster pace, roughly thirty seconds to a minute faster than you normally run. It will be hard and you'll feel uncomfortable, but focus on the finish and you'll get yourself to the end of the lap.

) Run one lap at a recovery pace, roughly the same pace as your warm up or even a bit slower.

) Repeat this cycle four times.

For a workout that combines mileage and speed training,

) Start with a 1.5-mile warm up and stretching.

) Run 3 to 4 miles at a faster pace, roughly 30 seconds to a minute faster than you'd normally run. If you're struggling, focus on putting your best effort into each of the faster-paced miles and reaching the finish line.

) Cool down for a mile afterward, and make sure to stretch.

to pavement, switch it up with grass or trails.) *After a short warm up, run hard for the length of one song on your playlist. During the next song, run at a . . .*

Training Charts

The hardest parts of running are making time for it and implementing a plan that works for you. No matter what kind of race you're preparing for, make sure your goals are reachable and that you have the time and ability to do the training you need to do. If you don't do the right work beforehand, you'll find yourself anxious, unprepared, and maybe even injured on race day. That's not the kind of fun and healthy racing experience you're aiming for.

The following charts offer some guidelines for crafting your own personal training plan. Feel free to tailor these recommendations to fit your lifestyle. The first chart will help you train for 5K and 10K races. These races are all about getting out there and being consistent with your running to slowly increase your endurance and mileage. Whatever you do, don't skip the rest days. They're just as imperative to your training process as running days, because they give your body time to recover and keep you from burning out. If you feel like adding in a speed work session, I suggest doing it during your midweek long run.

SETTING S.M.A.R.T. GOALS

Writing down your goals will make them more real. You can write them in your journal or tape them up in a place you see often, like on your refrigerator or bathroom mirror. They'll motivate you to keep working, even when you're struggling. If you want to stay happy and healthy while training, all you have to do is make your goals SMART: Specific, Measurable, Achievable, Realistic, and Timely.

SPECIFIC—To keep yourself focused and accountable, make specific goals like "Complete a 5K in 3 months," rather than vague or broad goals like "Run more."

MEASURABLE—Measure your progress in a running journal or on an app, and choose specific progress dates to keep yourself on track. If you want to be able to run a mile and a half after one month of training, you can easily measure your progress toward that goal just by writing down dates, times, and distances.

ACHIEVABLE—You want to make goals you can actually achieve, instead of signing up for a marathon next weekend when you've never run a step in your life. That doesn't mean your goal should be super easy—you should have to push yourself to reach it—but if it's too hard, you might end up ignoring it or giving up altogether.

REALISTIC—Creating a realistic goal is important, because you can be sure you'll actually reap the rewards of your work. You want an accomplishment you can be proud of, not some lofty ideal you'll never actually reach.

TIMELY—Make your goals timely. If you're trying to train for a race too far in the future, you might end up procrastinating because you feel like you have plenty of time. Then when race day arrives, you'll be unprepared and unhappy. But if you set a larger long-term goal with smaller short-term goals to reach along the way, you'll be prepared for success, pride, and all the other rewards running has to offer.

...recovery pace. Complete four fast songs and four recovery songs. ❯ *Add some cycling into your fitness routine on a recovery or rest day, whether outdoors or at*

5K & 10K TRAINING SUGGESTIONS

DAY	SUGGESTED TIME/MILEAGE	TYPE OF RUN
MONDAY	Start your week off with a **RECOVERY RUN** to bounce back from your weekend long run. This run should be one-fourth as long as your weekend long run, so if you ran 40 minutes last weekend, run for 10 minutes today.	This should be a slower run at a comfortable pace. If you want to alternate between walking and running, feel free. Try to keep it at a 4:1 variation, where you're running 4 minutes and walking 1 minute.
TUESDAY	**REST DAY.** Unless you want to go to the gym or do some other type of cardio, take it easy.	
WEDNESDAY	This is your **LONGEST WEEKDAY RUN.** Take the length of your last weekend long run, divide it in half, and add in a walk to make up the difference. So if your weekend run was 40 minutes, today you'll run for 20 minutes and walk for 20 minutes.	Try to pick up the pace a little on this run—go at least a little faster than you do on your recovery pace. Focus on breathing and feeling relaxed.
THURSDAY	Perk up with a **RECOVERY RUN**. This should be about 1 to 3 miles or 15 to 45 minutes of running/walking.	Run slowly and steadily to get your blood flowing and legs moving again after yesterday's tougher workout.
FRIDAY	**REST DAY.** Make sure to stretch and foam roll to relieve soreness.	
SATURDAY OR SUNDAY	This is the **LONGEST AND MOST IMPORTANT RUN** in your training cycle. Take your mileage or time from last weekend's run and add half a mile to 1 mile, or 5 to 10 minutes. So if you started with 1 mile or 10 minutes, then this time shoot for 2 miles or 20 minutes. Then, next week, try for 2.5 miles or 25 minutes. Keep increasing your long run incrementally. If you do this run on Saturday, use Sunday as a rest day, and vice versa.	This run should be a little bit faster than your recovery run, but make sure you're able to keep your pace consistent the whole time. If you want to add speed intervals, this is the time to do it.

the gym, to give your legs a great workout without the high impact of running.   Try doing a ladder workout at the local track. After a warm up, run...

HALF MARATHON TRAINING TIPS

Training for a half marathon means you'll have to do a few longer runs during your training—sometimes up to 3 hours, depending on your pace. It's important to be realistic about your training commitments. A half marathon is a big deal, and depending on your starting mileage, it may take you a while to build up for this kind of race. Many people choose to train over a longer time frame, like three to four months, to make sure they have ample time to get comfortable with the distance. Give yourself enough time, and on race day, you'll be confident and ready for the challenge. It might take a while, and you might have to make sacrifices to fit your training runs into your schedule, but in the end, you'll marvel at what you're capable of.

DAY	SUGGESTED TIME/MILEAGE	TYPE OF RUN
MONDAY	**REST DAY.** Rest days give your body a chance to recuperate and get stronger.	
TUESDAY	Go for a relatively **EASY RUN, BETWEEN 2 AND 5 MILES**.	This run will keep your legs loose for your workout the following day. Run at a pace a little bit faster than your recovery pace.
WEDNESDAY	Try an **INTERVAL WORKOUT** to build your speed. Warm up for 1 to 2 miles, then run at a faster (but consistent) pace for 2 to 3 miles. Finish with a cool-down run of 1 to 2 miles.	The warm up and cool-down should be at an easy pace, but run faster during the workout portion of the run. You should feel like you're pushing yourself.
THURSDAY	Go for a **3- TO 5-MILE RECOVERY RUN**.	This is an easier run at a slower, more relaxed pace than your other training runs.
FRIDAY	**REST DAY.** Even though you're not running, stretch out and foam roll to help with any soreness. Take it easy at night, because you have a long run ahead of you tomorrow.	
SATURDAY	This is the **LONGEST AND MOST IMPORTANT RUN** in your training cycle. Take the longest distance you can comfortably run and add 1 mile each week. Before you know it, you'll be running 10 miles for your long run!	This run should be a little bit faster than your recovery run, but make sure you're able to keep your pace consistent over the entire run.
SUNDAY	Since yesterday was your long run, today you'll need to do a **2- TO 5-MILE RECOVERY RUN.**	This is a relatively easy run at a relaxed pace.

...a 200-meter sprint, then 300 meters, 400 meters, back down to 300, and finally 200. Then cool down.   *The stair machine at your gym can give you a hill*

WHAT'S YOUR FAVORITE WAY TO VARY UP YOUR TRAINING ROUTINE?

Mary Kate Cornell

Even the most seasoned runner needs to change up his or her running routine once in a while! I've run seven marathons and dozens of half marathons, and while I LOVE running, it can get tedious. I have a few different strategies I fall back on when I get into a running rut and need to change it up.

One quick way I like to mix up my running routine is to get new running gear. Whether it's new shoes, fun capris, or a new gadget, testing out your new stuff makes any run a little bit more fun! Another quick way to mix it up is to run a new route. Maybe run your normal route backwards, find a trail you've been meaning to check out, or drive to another city after work and run there. Social media, especially Twitter and Instagram, is a great way to see where other runners in the area like to go. Then you can check out MapMyRun.com to plan out the best route.

One of my favorite ways to mix up the miles is to run with a buddy. Finding a good fit in a running buddy is also key. If you're a big talker, having a friend who likes to listen is great. Since I'm not as much of a talker when I run, I love having a buddy who can do most of the chatting so I only need to chime in when necessary. Running with brand new people is always fun, too. Sometimes the unknown can add an extra fun element to the run. I get nervous I won't be fast enough to keep up or I'll need to stop, but then before I know it, the pace evens out and my new friend wants to stop for water, too. Running buddies are also great motivators to help you get up and out early for your morning run. I can barely do it without having someone to meet up with.

While training for my most recent marathon, Mountains 2 Beach, I really wanted to break four hours for the first time. I'd attempted it six times before but couldn't get over the hump. Finally, I began to change up the types of runs I was doing.

Generally, I would go out and put in the mileage I'd planned for myself and call it a day, but when training for this race, I began to try out speed work a few times a week. As I saw progress each week and my mile times begin to drop, this training method got more and more fun. Now I love doing different types of runs each week, whether it's speed work, track workouts, or long runs. Making each one a little different goes a long way when you're working through a training cycle or you're in a little slump.

Having some strategies in your back pocket to help motivate you will help you stick to any running plan and get your mojo back.

workout without the hill.. ❱ After each mile, do a set of walking lunges for one minute, then continue your run. ❱ Quality over quantity! If you're feeling sluggish . . .

HIT THE ROAD **87**

Hill Training

Running up and down hills can be intimidating, but it's a great way for runners to train. Running in the hills complements the running you're doing on flat ground by working different muscles. For example, hills are great for developing the strong, dependable quadriceps you need for running long distances even on completely flat ground.

Plus, it's hard to find completely flat ground to run on. If you add hills to your normal training, you'll be ready to face them when they pop up along the course on race day.

While running hills, focus on taking one step at a time. As you start up the hill, shorten your stride. You won't be able to keep the same pace that you were using on flat ground, but try to keep the same rhythm. Steady your breathing and stand up straight. Look at the top of the hill and remind yourself that you can get there.

Once you reach the top of the hill, don't stop! A handy tip from my old cross-country coach: Count to 10 as you crest the hill. Once you're done counting, you'll have naturally fallen back into your normal running pace. Your breathing will slow back down, and you'll be able to keep going.

FAR vs. FAST

Running fast and running far are very different goals, and they'll challenge you to push past your limits in different ways. Short, fast runs are great for building muscle quickly and bumping up your metabolism, but they're also more likely to give you injuries. Long, slower runs don't make your muscles as strong, but they build your endurance and injure you less often.

TO WORK ON RUNNING FASTER, you'll need to gradually introduce speed workouts (see page 83) into your training. Focus on short bursts of speed that increase your "leg turnover," or the amount of time it takes for your leg to take a step. In the beginning, these short bursts may only be 15 to 30 seconds, but soon you'll be able to make these intervals last for minutes and then for miles. It'll be a challenge to start running faster, especially if you're a beginner to speed training. Focus on breathing and relaxing during the faster intervals. A stopwatch or app can help you keep track of exactly how much time has passed during an interval and how long you have left.

RUNNING FAR is great because it increases endurance, which will help you continue to tack on the miles. Distance training takes patience and time. Long runs can get boring, and by definition they take up a larger portion of your day. But as your mileage increases, you'll be proud of your accomplishments and gain self-confidence—not to mention all the benefits to your metabolism, heart rate, and overall health.

Once you learn what works for your body and mind, you'll be able to add both speed and distance work into your training plan, depending on your goals and aspirations as a runner. And remember: When you're just beginning, it's important to focus on the small accomplishments. If you can't run very fast or far yet, don't worry. You'll get there before you know it.

. . . it's okay to cut your run short and take a rest day. ❱ *Many apps include running workouts with voice cues that tell you when to speed up and slow down.*

Your Running Journal

A running journal can be a valuable source of motivation and accountability. Writing down your training stats can help you gain insight into your progress. It's inspirational to page back through your journal and see how far you've come since two, four, or six months ago. You get to see the work you've put into running and how it's paying off. Having something to look back on while you make your schedule for the next week is also helpful. You can tweak certain things that you didn't enjoy and make sure to continue doing things you liked.

Additionally, after a hard run, having a place to write down your emotions can be very cathartic. You can release any negativity you feel about running at that moment and start your next run with a clean slate. A journal can also help you discern which foods work for your body before a long run and which to stay away from. Starting on page 101, I'll give you a few sample journal pages to get started.

Write as much or as little as you want—no one else has to see it. Or, if you do want to share it, you could publish it online for friends, family, or other runners from around the world to read. I started my blog because no one else in my life ran, and no one really understood why I wanted to put myself through the training for my first half marathon. But through my blog, I joined an online community of people who understood my love of running deeply and who encouraged and supported one another's running goals. And when I go back and read my early blog posts about training for my first half marathon, it still makes me feel proud of my accomplishments.

> **Good things come slow— especially in distance running.**
>
> BILL DELLINGER,
> MIDDLE-DISTANCE RUNNER

⟩ Set milestones to hit at certain times along your route. For instance, "I'll run to the Starbucks, and if I can make it there in 12 minutes, I'll get a glass of water."

7
LET'S RACE

"Once you make the decision that you will not fail, your heart and body will follow."

KARA GOUCHER,
LONG-DISTANCE RUNNER

The Starting Line

Waking up on the morning of a big race is one of the most exhilarating feelings I've ever experienced, but it can also be nerve-racking. What if you forget something? What if something goes wrong? To help allay your fears, plan ahead and prepare everything you'll need the evening before the race.

Lay out clothes you've trained in so you can be sure you'll feel comfortable throughout the run. If you're traveling for your race, pack your suitcase using a list so you won't forget anything. If you do forget something important, like your lucky pair of socks or the special breakfast you planned to eat before the race, don't let it mess with your attitude and plan. Focus on the positive and what you're about to accomplish. Sweating the small stuff won't help, and this is supposed to be fun.

When it comes to the actual race, if you've done your training, you have nothing to worry about. Once you start running, your adrenaline will take you to the finish line. If you're nervous, focus on how far you've come and use that nervous energy to propel you forward. Your training will give you the tools you need to take care of the rest.

All that stands between you and the finish line is yourself. Keep a positive mindset and focus on putting one foot in front of the other. Even when things get difficult during the race, trust in the fact that you've put in the work. In many ways, you've already accomplished the goal of committing to a healthier lifestyle, and this is just a victory lap.

CONGRATS—YOU'VE REACHED THE FINISH LINE! HERE ARE A FEW POST-RACE TIPS TO HELP YOUR BODY RECOVER AND TO KEEP THE BUZZ GOING:

Fuel Your Race

What you eat in preparation for a race can have a big impact on your performance. Many races offer a "carbo-load" dinner before a race, and many runners take part in the festivities. It's fun to get together with other people who'll be running the race with you, but keep in mind that doing something out of your routine may mess up your stomach. You may want to stick to what you've done throughout your training so you can be confident you'll feel good the next day.

One of the most important things to do in the days leading up to your race is to make sure you're drinking a lot of water. You should always be making a conscious effort to drink more water, but it's especially important as your race approaches. Carry a water bottle around with you and take sips throughout the day to keep your body extra hydrated and prepared.

The night before the race, eat something you're familiar with. If you like high-carb foods, go with an option like the pizza recipe on page 70 or the pasta recipe on page 69. It'll keep you full, and it'll serve as great fuel for your race. Stay away from spicy foods, or you may upset your stomach, especially if you're feeling any anxiety about the race. Try not to take any abnormal supplements, medications, or anything else that may rile up your digestive system. Change before a race is never a good idea.

On the morning of the race, stick to something light. This is not the time to wing it and hope things work out. Don't add coffee to your routine if you're not used to drinking coffee before you run. When I travel for races, I sometimes pack peanut butter, jelly, and bread so I can make a sandwich in the morning per my usual routine. The Whole-Grain Sweet Potato and Buttermilk Muffins recipe on page 64 is a great breakfast option.

Remember to avoid too much sugar, dairy, and soda on the days leading up to your race, as they can all affect your body, especially your stomach, in a negative way. Try to eat healthy and normal instead of splurging on your meals because you expect to burn the calories during the race. Putting on weight the week leading up to the big day will only throw off your performance.

Once you've completed your race, celebrate with a few extra treats, like the Chocolate Chunk Almond Cookies with protein powder on page 75. It's normal for your stomach to be a little off, especially if you just completed a long-distance race, so don't overdo it if you're not feeling well.

If you're sore, fill a bathtub with ice water, and submerge your body in it for 10 minutes. Remember to move your toes and ankles around.. ❭ *Drink a lot of . . .*

During the Race

Do your research before the race so you know where to pick up your race-day number—sometimes this happens the day of the race, sometimes a few days before. Try to be aware of any road closures or traffic issues on race morning as well, because you may not be able to take your normal route to the start.

As you head to the starting line of your race, whether you're running with 25 or 25,000 people, think about all the training you've done. You've got this. Check to see if they have pacers anywhere or signs that direct you to line up according to pace. If you're not super fast, don't line up in the front. If you'll be doing any walking, stay toward the back. It's better to start in the back and pass people on your way forward than start in the front and get in the way of faster runners.

You'll probably have a lot of adrenaline flowing through your body at the start line. This can work to your advantage, as long as you know how to harness it. Don't take off too fast—you may feel fatigue well before you should because you used up all your energy right at the beginning. But do let the excitement carry you. Just remind yourself to relax and run your race.

Perhaps the most important thing to remember about race day is to enjoy it. Pause for a moment to take a deep breath and remember how much you love what you're doing. Pump your fists as you pass the crowds. Take in all the funny signs people are holding. They're cheering for you! It's supposed to make you smile, so soak it in.

As you near the finish line, give it everything you have. You'll be able to run much faster than you expected because of the excitement you feel and the encouragement you get from the crowds. Make a face as you cross the finish line—they usually have photographers taking pictures.

GEAR CHECK & THROWAWAY CLOTHES

Many races offer a "gear check," or an area where you can store your items while you run. The race organizers provide a plastic bag with your number on it so you can claim it after the race. This is a great way to keep a sweatshirt with you until the last minute or store an extra T-shirt for after the race. If you drive yourself, you may want to check your wallet or keys, but gear-check bags can get stolen or misplaced, so don't put anything too valuable in there.

Throwaway clothes are another option if it's a bit chilly in the morning but you know you'll get warm as soon as you start running. When the gun goes off, many people shed old sweaters or thrift-store jackets that they don't want heating them up or weighting them down during the race. Many races collect the throwaway clothes found at the starting line and donate them to local shelters and charities.

. . . water—your body exerted a lot of effort during the race. ❱ *Do some light walking to keep your blood flowing. It's counterintuitive, but sitting down will only make*

WHAT DO YOU LOVE ABOUT RACING?

Bridget Durkin

What I love about racing is that you never really know what is going to happen on race day. A personal best? A personal worst? Or just an OK performance but finishing with a smile on your face? You will never know until you cross the finish line. Personally, I have had more "good" races than "bad" races. In my two years of consistent running, I have managed to run a personal record (PR) six times in the half marathon distance, and it helps to start as a beginner runner. Now I am always wondering leading up to race day, "Can I get a new PR?" This is where I have gained the most joy out of running and even racing. Knowing the work you put into training, even on the bad days, will eventually pay off.

One thing that keeps me motivated is having a race or two on the calendar. I need something to work towards. So I will pick one as "the race" where I incorporate speed workouts and really focus on a PR during my training. I also will mix in races for purely fun with no expectations. One race in particular is very special to me, The Mammoth Half Marathon. I only had one goal in mind, which was to help my sister run her first half marathon. I will never forget the experience and the emotions we shared together at the finish line.

Each race I learn something new about myself and about the sport; my level of fitness, how prepared I was, and how hard I can push myself—sometimes to the point of throwing up at the finish line: it has happened twice! But the absolute best part of racing is that feeling at the end, which consist of feeling tired, happy, sweaty, joyful, accomplished, achy, energized, grateful, sick yet starving, but definitely ready to celebrate, and that keeps me coming back for more.

you sorer. ❭ Make sure to take some time off to let your body recover after a race. Enjoy a week of no running. ❭ Celebrate! You've just completed something . . .

LET'S RACE **95**

LEADING UP TO YOUR RACE

Before a race, create a list of things you need to do, whether it's finishing a project at work, packing your bags, washing your favorite sports bra, or texting your friends directions to the finish line. If you take care of things beforehand, you'll feel more prepared and relaxed for the race. Here's a sample list of things you can do so that the only thing you're worried about on race day is running your best.

⟩ Wash your race-day clothes, including your socks, sports bra, underwear, shirt, and shorts.

⟩ Pick up your bib number.

⟩ Charge any electronics you may be taking with you, such as your cell phone, tracking watch, or music player.

⟩ Update your race-day playlist with music to get you through the miles.

⟩ Confirm your ride to the start line if you need one.

⟩ Find out if the race tracks runners, and let friends and family who may want to track you know about this option.

THE NIGHT BEFORE THE RACE

Relax—you've got a race ahead of you! This day should be a fairly low-key, as you'll need a lot of energy in the morning. Try to stay off your feet and legs, don't do anything out of the ordinary, and make sure you stretch before bed. Here are some other things you can do to prepare the night before a race:

⟩ Lay out your clothes, along with your headphones and any fuel you're taking with you. Include your bib and timing chip if you've picked them up.

⟩ Visualize yourself crossing the finish line.

⟩ Remind anyone who may be coming to watch about the approximate time you expect to finish and where you'll meet them after the race.

⟩ Remember to drink a lot of water and eat a good dinner.

⟩ Set at least three alarms for the following morning.

> **❝ Most people run a race to see who is fastest. I run a race to see who has the most guts. ❞**
> STEVE PREFONTAINE,
> OLYMPIC RUNNER

. . . amazing. Relish in your achievements and drink a glass of bubbly. ⟩ Stretch and foam roll. This gets blood flowing to your muscles and helps you recover faster.

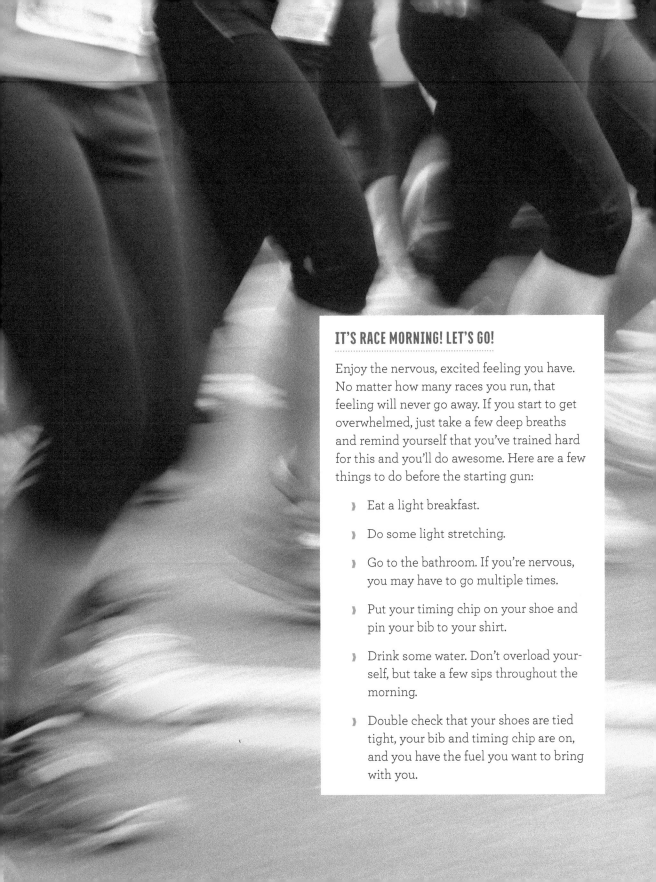

IT'S RACE MORNING! LET'S GO!

Enjoy the nervous, excited feeling you have. No matter how many races you run, that feeling will never go away. If you start to get overwhelmed, just take a few deep breaths and remind yourself that you've trained hard for this and you'll do awesome. Here are a few things to do before the starting gun:

❯ Eat a light breakfast.

❯ Do some light stretching.

❯ Go to the bathroom. If you're nervous, you may have to go multiple times.

❯ Put your timing chip on your shoe and pin your bib to your shirt.

❯ Drink some water. Don't overload yourself, but take a few sips throughout the morning.

❯ Double check that your shoes are tied tight, your bib and timing chip are on, and you have the fuel you want to bring with you.

Half Marathon & Marathon Races

If you've decided to tackle a long-distance run like a half or full marathon, there are a few extra details to take into account.

Your training will, of course, be more extensive, because the distances you're running will be longer. Also, both of these distances will require you to take fuel while running, so your training will need to include that. You don't want to be halfway through your first marathon when you find out your stomach doesn't tolerate energy gel.

In the last few weeks before your race, your training mileage will go down as you rest your body in anticipation of the race. Many people struggle through this time, because they've grown accustomed to running more miles and they feel like these shorter distances aren't adequately preparing them to finish the race. They start to have phantom injuries and become grouchy in a weird but common side effect of marathon training often referred to as "taper tantrums."

Longer-distance races usually involve more logistics than shorter ones, so make sure you're prepared. In the weeks leading up to your race, check the race website to find out when and where to pick up your bib and how to get to the start line. Make a list of the things you need to take along, and if you're traveling to the race, use that list to pack your bags a few days beforehand. That way, you'll have time to pick up anything you might need, especially the fuel you've trained with. If you're traveling by airplane, make sure to bring your running shoes with you in a carry-on, just in case your luggage gets lost. You can always buy new clothes at the last minute, but not having your own shoes for these long distances can make the race very difficult.

Running a half or full marathon can be one of the most amazing and rewarding experiences of your life. It takes a lot of time to train for, and you'll go through a wave of emotions leading up to race day, but with the proper training, it's more than worth it. You'll push and challenge yourself in ways you never thought possible, and the fact that you'll be a marathoner at the finish line is something that no one can ever take away from you. As you push off from the starting line, trust your training and believe in yourself.

. . . What are you waiting for? This book is almost over. **GET OUT THERE AND RUN!**

98 RUNNING FOR WOMEN

RUNNING JOURNAL

Use this journal to record what works best for you before, during, and after running. If you keep up with it, you can look back during future training rounds to see which approaches were the most helpful (or unhelpful) to you in the past. Keeping track of how far you've come is a great way to stay motivated and accountable.

DATE: **TIME:**

DISTANCE RUN:

HEART RATE:

TYPE OF RUN:

FOOD NOTES:

HOW I FELT BEFORE:

HOW I FELT DURING:

HOW I FELT AFTER:

WHAT TO FOCUS ON NEXT RUN:

EXTRA COMMENTS & MOTIVATION:

DATE: **TIME:**

DISTANCE RUN:

HEART RATE:

TYPE OF RUN:

FOOD NOTES:

HOW I FELT BEFORE:

HOW I FELT DURING:

HOW I FELT AFTER:

WHAT TO FOCUS ON NEXT RUN:

EXTRA COMMENTS & MOTIVATION:

DATE: **TIME:**

DISTANCE RUN:

HEART RATE:

TYPE OF RUN:

FOOD NOTES:

HOW I FELT BEFORE:

HOW I FELT DURING:

HOW I FELT AFTER:

WHAT TO FOCUS ON NEXT RUN:

EXTRA COMMENTS & MOTIVATION:

DATE: **TIME:**
....

DISTANCE RUN:
....

HEART RATE:
....

TYPE OF RUN:
....

FOOD NOTES:
....

HOW I FELT BEFORE:
....

HOW I FELT DURING:
....

HOW I FELT AFTER:
....

WHAT TO FOCUS ON NEXT RUN:
....

EXTRA COMMENTS & MOTIVATION:

....

DATE: **TIME:**
....

DISTANCE RUN:
....

HEART RATE:
....

TYPE OF RUN:
....

FOOD NOTES:
....

HOW I FELT BEFORE:
....

HOW I FELT DURING:
....

HOW I FELT AFTER:
....

WHAT TO FOCUS ON NEXT RUN:
....

EXTRA COMMENTS & MOTIVATION:

....

DATE: **TIME:**

DISTANCE RUN:

HEART RATE:

TYPE OF RUN:

FOOD NOTES:

HOW I FELT BEFORE:

HOW I FELT DURING:

HOW I FELT AFTER:

WHAT TO FOCUS ON NEXT RUN:

EXTRA COMMENTS & MOTIVATION:

DATE: **TIME:**

DISTANCE RUN:

HEART RATE:

TYPE OF RUN:

FOOD NOTES:

HOW I FELT BEFORE:

HOW I FELT DURING:

HOW I FELT AFTER:

WHAT TO FOCUS ON NEXT RUN:

EXTRA COMMENTS & MOTIVATION:

DATE: TIME:
....

DISTANCE RUN:
....

HEART RATE:
....

TYPE OF RUN:
....

FOOD NOTES:
....

HOW I FELT BEFORE:
....

HOW I FELT DURING:
....

HOW I FELT AFTER:
....

WHAT TO FOCUS ON NEXT RUN:
....

EXTRA COMMENTS & MOTIVATION:

....

DATE: TIME:
....

DISTANCE RUN:
....

HEART RATE:
....

TYPE OF RUN:
....

FOOD NOTES:
....

HOW I FELT BEFORE:
....

HOW I FELT DURING:
....

HOW I FELT AFTER:
....

WHAT TO FOCUS ON NEXT RUN:
....

EXTRA COMMENTS & MOTIVATION:

....

DATE: **TIME:**

DISTANCE RUN:

HEART RATE:

TYPE OF RUN:

FOOD NOTES:

HOW I FELT BEFORE:

HOW I FELT DURING:

HOW I FELT AFTER:

WHAT TO FOCUS ON NEXT RUN:

EXTRA COMMENTS & MOTIVATION:

DATE: **TIME:**

DISTANCE RUN:

HEART RATE:

TYPE OF RUN:

FOOD NOTES:

HOW I FELT BEFORE:

HOW I FELT DURING:

HOW I FELT AFTER:

WHAT TO FOCUS ON NEXT RUN:

EXTRA COMMENTS & MOTIVATION:

DATE: **TIME:**

DISTANCE RUN:

HEART RATE:

TYPE OF RUN:

FOOD NOTES:

HOW I FELT BEFORE:

HOW I FELT DURING:

HOW I FELT AFTER:

WHAT TO FOCUS ON NEXT RUN:

EXTRA COMMENTS & MOTIVATION:

DATE: **TIME:**

DISTANCE RUN:

HEART RATE:

TYPE OF RUN:

FOOD NOTES:

HOW I FELT BEFORE:

HOW I FELT DURING:

HOW I FELT AFTER:

WHAT TO FOCUS ON NEXT RUN:

EXTRA COMMENTS & MOTIVATION:

RESOURCES

BOOKS

Armstrong, Kristin. *Mile Markers: The 26.2 Most Important Reasons Why Women Run*. New York, NY: Rodale, Inc., 2011.

Heminsley, Alexandra. *Running Like a Girl: Notes on Learning to Run*. New York, NY: Simon & Schuster, 2013.

McDougall, Christopher. *Born to Run: A Hidden Tribe, Superathletes, and the Greatest Race the World Has Never Seen*. New York, NY: Vintage Press, 2011.

Murakami, Haruki. *What I Talk About When I Talk About Running*. New York, NY: Vintage Press, 2009.

Scott, Dagny. *Runner's World Complete Book of Women's Running*. New York, NY: Rodale, Inc., 2000.

Sheehan, George. *Running & Being: The Total Experience*. New York, NY: Rodale, Inc., 2014.

WEBSITES

www.runnersworld.com

www.webmd.com

www.mayoclinic.com/first-aid

blog.walkjogrun.net

www.babygearlab.com

www.running.competitor.com

www.livestrong.com

www.chirunning.com

www.runneracademy.com

www.fitnessmagazine.com

www.active.com

www.prevention.com

REFERENCES

Dada, Janice H. "Marathon Fueling — Runners Need Proper Nutrition and Hydration for the 26.2-Mile Stretch." *Today's Dietician* 12, no. 3 (March 2010): 36. www.todaysdietitian.com/newarchives/030810p36.shtml.

Institute of Medicine. "Dietary Reference Intakes for Energy, Carbohydrate, Fiber, Fat, Fatty Acids, Cholesterol, Protein, and Amino Acids." September 5, 2002. iom.nationalacademies.org/Reports/2002/Dietary-Reference-Intakes-for-Energy-Carbohydrate-Fiber-Fat-Fatty-Acids-Cholesterol-Protein-and-Amino-Acids.aspx.

U.S. Department of Agriculture and U.S. Department of Health and Human Services. "Dietary Guidelines for Americans 2010. " Page 24. www.cnpp.usda.gov/sites/default/files/dietary_guidelines_for_americans/PolicyDoc.pdf

INDEX

CPSIA information can be obtained
at www.ICGtesting.com
Printed in the USA
LVHW02s2002281117
557702LV00002B/2/P